Studying the
New Testament

Studying the New Testament

Morna D. Hooker

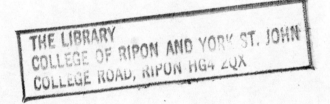
London EPWORTH PRESS

7162 0340 5

Enquiries should be addressed to
The Methodist Publishing House
Wellington Road
Wimbledon
London SW19 8EU
Printed in Great Britain by
The Garden City Press Limited
Letchworth, Hertfordshire SG6 1JS

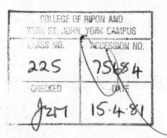

Contents

Note for Methodist Local Preachers on trial studying for the Connexional Examination in the New Testament

Studying the New Testament is a companion volume to *Groundwork of Biblical Studies* and the student, whether taking a correspondence course or not, should note the Study Scheme printed at the end of this book. Examination questions may be set on the whole of *Studying the New Testament*. The chapters from *Groundwork of Biblical Studies* referred to in the Study Scheme should be carefully read as they provide essential background knowledge.

Introduction

THIS book has been written as a textbook for Methodist Local Preachers on trial, but it is hoped that others may find it a useful guide in studying the New Testament. When used in conjunction with the companion volume, *Groundwork of Biblical Studies,* it offers a scheme for working through the New Testament in twelve studies. Each chapter provides the outline of a study, together with comments on selected passages. It is, of course, impossible to cover the whole of the New Testament in such a course, but it is hoped that the passages which have been selected for study will serve to indicate the most important issues, and suggest possibilities for further study. At the end of each chapter there are suggestions for further reading. More difficult books are marked with an asterisk. Questions on each chapter will be found in the Study Scheme at the end of the book.

In addition to the sections of *Groundwork of Biblical Studies* which are included in the study outline there are others which should be referred to when need arises. Students are unlikely, for example, to want to read through a catalogue of the 'Cities of St. Paul', but will find this chapter useful when reading Paul's letters or the Acts of the Apostles. Sections which will be found useful for reference are:

10 l-s The History of the Biblical Period
14 a–b, g–k The Ancient Manuscripts
27 Temple and Synagogue
33 Jewish Sects and Parties
35 Cities of St. Paul
36 New Testament Chronology

Chapter 1

The Good News about Jesus

Passages for special study:
Romans *1*.3 f.
1 Corinthians *15*.1–8.
Mark *1*.1–13.
Matthew *1–2*.
Luke *1–2*.
John *1*.1–18; *20*.31.

THE first problem which confronts us, when we come to study the New Testament, is to know where to begin. It might seem natural to follow the advice given to Alice and begin at the beginning. But although Matthew's gospel was placed first in the canon (see *Groundwork* 13a) because it was once thought to be the earliest of our four gospels, it is now generally believed to be based on Mark, so that if we are going to begin our study with the gospels, we should clearly look first at Mark. Once we decide, however, to begin with one of our twenty-seven documents because it was written earlier than another, we raise all sorts of problems, for the earliest sections of the New Testament are the letters of St. Paul. Should we perhaps begin there? For a number of reasons we have chosen to begin with the gospels—chiefly because Pauline theology is tough meat for the beginner. It must not be forgotten, however, that Paul was preaching and writing *before* the evangelists wrote their gospels, even though, of course, the tradition used in the gospels may have existed in Paul's day.

This means that if we want to study the earliest written summary of Christian belief, we shall have to look at Paul's letters, and it is worth drawing attention to one or two places where Paul reminds his hearers of what he had preached to them, before we turn our attention to the gospels. 'Reminds' them, because of course Paul is writing to those who are already Christians: he does not need to explain the gospel at length. Thus we find Paul writing to the Corinthians in 1 Cor. *15*:

> Now I would remind you, brethren, in what terms I preached to you the gospel, which you received, in which you stand, by which you are saved, if you hold it fast—unless you believed in vain.
>
> For I delivered to you as of first importance what I also received, that Christ died for our sins in accordance with the scriptures, that he was buried, that he was raised on the third day in accordance with the scriptures, and that he appeared to Cephas, then to the twelve. Then he appeared to more than five hundred brethren at one time, most of whom are still alive, though some have fallen asleep. Then he appeared to James, then to all the apostles. Last of all, as to one untimely born, he appeared also to me.

Paul's summary of the gospel here is very brief. More than half of it is taken up with a summary of the appearances of the Risen Lord. There is a good reason for this, for Paul is concerned in this chapter with the question of resurrection, and he therefore sets out the evidence for the appearances of the Risen Christ in some detail. Even so, he does not tell us the stories of these appearances—not even the one which he himself experienced. We need to turn to Acts to read about this. Paul contents himself with giving a list.

Straight away, then, we notice two interesting things about Paul's summary of the gospel. First, it is 'geared into' the particular situation to which he is writing: he emphasizes one point because it is relevant to his argument. It is typical of Paul, when he is referring to the gospel, to state it in a way which demonstrates its relevance to the matter in hand. Secondly, it is typical of Paul that he does not spell out what happened when Christ 'appeared'. We look in vain in Paul's letters for stories about Jesus: the one exception—recounted for a very good reason—is the account of the Last Supper in 1 Cor. *11*.

Apart from the list of appearances, Paul's summary of the gospel consists of four brief statements: 'Christ died . . . he was buried . . . he was raised . . . he appeared.' We have here four events—or rather two, since the burial and the appearances serve to confirm the reality of the death and resurrection. It is possible that Paul is quoting a traditional formula here: if so, we have one of the earliest Christian 'creeds'. A creed records not only facts, but beliefs about their significance. Notice how already here the statements regarding the central events of Christ's death and resurrection contain interpretation: they are both 'in accordance with the scriptures', and Christ's death is 'for our sins'.

Another 'mini-creed' can be found in Rom. *1*.3 f. Here, Paul is introducing himself to the Christians in Rome: although he has not yet visited the city he regards himself as their pastor, because he has been called to be an apostle to the Gentiles. He is commissioned to preach

The gospel concerning God's Son, who was descended from David according to the flesh and designated Son of God in power according to the Spirit of holiness by his resurrection from the dead, Jesus Christ our Lord.

This time Paul's summary of the gospel is a little more elaborate. It is, we learn, about God's Son. In human terms ('according to the flesh') he is the Son of David, i.e. the Messiah or Christ of Jewish hopes. But he has been proclaimed Son of God by his resurrection from the dead. Notice how, this time, the reference to the death of Christ is almost incidental. We are, however, told something very significant about the resurrection. By raising Christ from the dead God vindicated him, declared him to be in the right, acknowledged him as his Son. It was through the resurrection that the disciples came to believe in Jesus as God's Son, and to acknowledge him as their Lord.

Turning from these two brief summaries of the gospel to

11

the books which we know as 'gospels', we are clearly dealing with something rather different. We are so used to the term 'gospel' that we are inclined to forget that it really means simply 'good news', and that it came to be applied to our four gospels because they set out the good news about Jesus Christ. The term proved a useful one to describe a form of literature which has no parallels elsewhere. There are no other books like our four gospels, for they do not pretend to be straightforward history, and they are certainly not intended to be works of fiction: rather they are attempts to set out the significance of the life and death of Jesus, who was Son of David according to the flesh, and was declared Son of God in power by the resurrection from the dead.

Mark's 'Prologue': *1*.1–13

When Mark set out to write his gospel he was, as far as we know, doing something which no one before him had done. How did he set about his task? Most of the material which he used came to him in the form of short units—e.g. a story about a miracle, or about the Transfiguration, or perhaps a parable. What Mark had to do was to fit these various stories together. There were various ways in which he could do this. One was simply to string the stories together in any order, without bothering what kind of stories they were—and occasionally one has the impression that Mark (or someone before him) has done precisely that. Another was to sort out the material into various piles according to their theme—to put a group of parables together, e.g. (as in ch. *4*), or a group of stories which show Jesus in conflict with the authorities (as in ch. *2*). Another was to set out the stories in chronological order, as happens when we come to the passion narrative. It may seem as though this last was Mark's normal method, because we tend to think of things as belonging to the 'beginning' or the 'end' of Jesus' ministry, but of course what we are really thinking of is the place where Mark has put them; it is unlikely that many of the stories came to him with any kind of 'date' attached to them. A final method of arranging the material was to set it out in such a way that the arrangement

12

itself helps the reader to grasp the meaning of the gospel. We shall see, in future studies, that Mark has in fact arranged his material in a very skilful way, so that as we read his gospel we are confronted with the authority of Jesus, challenged to become his disciples, taught what it means to follow him, and finally brought to understand how it was that it was only through his death that Jesus came to be acknowledged as Son of God.

Mark was writing, however, for those who knew 'the gospel' already. His book has something of the flavour of a detective story, with all the characters (apart from the central one) more or less in the dark; yet he realizes that his readers know the end of the story, and do not need to turn to the last page to learn the explanation. In these circumstances, the wise author will adopt a bold course of action and take his readers into his confidence from the beginning: if he sets out the full solution in the first chapter, then his readers are able to enjoy picking up the clues in the narrative which are obscure to the characters in the story, but perfectly clear to those who are in the know. Now this is, in effect, what Mark has done. For if we read the opening verses of his gospel, we shall be in no doubt as to who Jesus is, and why he acts in the way he does. But if we begin reading the story at *1*.14, trying to put ourselves into the shoes of someone who has never heard it before, we shall find ourselves as astonished as the disciples, crowds and religious leaders at the extraordinary words and actions of this strange Galilean preacher. Mark has used the story of John the Baptist, together with the accounts of Jesus' baptism and temptation, to set out vital information about the person of Jesus.

Let us look more closely at the way in which he has done this. He lets the cat out of the bag straight away, of course, in his opening words, which we should probably understand as a title: 'The beginning of the gospel of Jesus Christ, the Son of God'. After this, the very first thing he gives us is a quotation from the Old Testament (a combination of Mal. *3*.1 and Isa. *40*.3—Mark gets his reference slightly wrong). Mark begins in this way because he wished to make clear that the events which he is going on to describe are the fulfilment of Old

Testament promises: if John the Baptist is the messenger who prepares the way, then the one who follows must be the Lord.

This, of course, is why Mark is interested in John, and why he begins his 'gospel' with the story of John. The Baptist is not important in himself, but only as a witness to Jesus. He prepares the way of the one who follows him by preaching repentance—and the whole population flocks to hear him and be baptized. If Mark describes what John ate and wore, this is so that we may recognize him for what he is—a man of the wilderness, and a prophet like Elijah (cf. Zech. *13*.4 and 2 Kgs. *1*.8). As for his preaching, Mark records only words which point forward to Jesus—to the mightier one who follows John, who will baptize with the Holy Spirit instead of with water. Although Mark's first paragraph seems to be about John, then, his real concern is with Jesus: John is introduced only as a signpost to indicate the significance of his successor.

So Jesus arrives on the scene and is baptized, identifying himself with those who await the salvation of God. It was at this point, Mark tells us, that Jesus saw the Spirit descending on him, and heard a voice from heaven. Mark does not suggest that anyone else saw or heard anything unusual—not even John. It is only we, the readers, who are privileged to be told the real significance of what is happening: Jesus has been acknowledged by God as his Son, and whatever he now does will be done in the power of God's creative Spirit. The words spoken from heaven remind us of a number of Old Testament passages which speak of God's choice of Israel to be his people. In particular, they echo Ps. *2*.7, where the words 'You are my Son' are addressed to the king, as representative of his people.

But the first thing that the Spirit does is to drive Jesus into the wilderness for forty days—the place where Israel spent forty years being tested (and failing miserably!). Mark's first readers would probably see a link with Israel straight away, for Israel had been chosen to be God's Son (cf. Hos. *11*.1). Now Jesus has taken over Israel's role: he has been acknowledged by God as his Son. His first act is to do battle with Satan. Strangely, Mark does not tell us here what the outcome

14

of this encounter was! However, as we read on through the gospel we shall see that, far from falling victim to Satan, Jesus has overcome Satan.

These three stories, then, are of special significance in the plan of Mark's gospel, because they give us vital information which helps us to understand the rest of the story. They provide us with Christological information—information, that is, about who Jesus is. Already we know that he is the Messiah, and the fulfilment of Old Testament promises; that he is greater than John the Baptist; that he is the Son of God, and well-pleasing to God; that the Holy Spirit rests upon him, and that he will himself baptize others with the Holy Spirit; that he has (so we may assume) resisted the temptation of Satan, and thus shown himself to be truly God's Son.

Matthew: *1–2*

We have seen that Mark had an excellent theological reason for beginning his account of the good news about Jesus with the story of John the Baptist. But this was by no means the only starting-place which he might have chosen—and both Matthew and Luke decided to begin somewhat differently. If we compare the outlines of our three Synoptic gospels (see *Groundwork* 28b–j), we find that both Matthew and Luke write two whole chapters before they reach the place where Mark begins his story, in *1*.2.

Matthew begins in a way which one might have thought was guaranteed to lose his readers' interest straight away. His first seventeen verses are taken up with the genealogy of Jesus, tracing his ancestry back to the time of the Exile in Babylon, beyond that to David, and finally to Abraham, the forefather of Israel. But Matthew has a good reason for beginning in this somewhat tedious way: his interest in Jesus' ancestry is not historical, but theological. The names on the family tree are not particularly important. What Matthew is trying to do is to show how God's plan for Israel has come to fulfilment: the periods of fourteen generations which link Jesus to the great events and great figures of the past show how he is the completion of God's purpose. For Matthew, it does not matter that this ancestry is traced through Joseph, and not Mary.

The story of Jesus' birth reflects Jewish marriage customs, whereby the ceremony of betrothal was a legal ceremony as binding as our wedding ceremony. Mary is described as a virgin, and is said to have conceived by the power of the Holy Spirit. Matthew sees this as a fulfilment of Old Testament scripture, but we see here an example of the way in which some of the Old Testament texts taken over by the Christians did not always fit very well. The passage which he quotes, Isa. 7.14, in fact uses a Hebrew word which means simply 'young woman'. It was the Septuagint—the Greek translation of the Old Testament—which used the Greek word for 'virgin' in that passage as the result of a misunderstanding. Moreover, the name given to the child in Isaiah was 'Immanuel', not 'Jesus'! Nevertheless, the name 'Immanuel' (or 'Emmanuel') is clearly an appropriate one for Matthew to apply to Jesus; he interpreted Isa. 7 in the light of his experience of Christ.

Many Christians today regard the birth narratives in Matthew and Luke as expressions of theological rather than historical truth: i.e. they are attempts to express, in ways familiar at the time, a fundamental belief about the person of Jesus. Whatever we decide on this particular point, the basic truth which underlies these stories, far more important than the manner of Jesus' birth, is the fact that in this event the Spirit of God was at work. Whether the birth of Jesus was 'miraculous' or 'normal', the eye of faith sees in it the creative activity of God.

Already, in the words of the angel (*1*.20 f.) and the quotation from scripture (*1*.23), Matthew has given us important information about Jesus. In his birth, the Holy Spirit is at work; his name, Jesus (which means 'he saves'), is an indication of what he will do; the name 'Emmanuel' ('God with us') belongs to him also. In the story of the wise men we are given further information. Jesus is said to have been born at Bethlehem, the city of King David, so fulfilling the prophecy of Mic. 5.2. Whether or not there were any wise men is a debatable question. It is pointless now to try to identify the 'star' or discuss how any celestial object could come to rest over a particular house. It is far more important to try to see what Matthew is wanting to say about Jesus in this story: for the wise men from the East who worship the child symbolize the Gentile nations who will one day acknowledge him as Lord. There is no other record of Herod's attempt to kill the child by slaughtering the infants in Bethlehem, though the action is in character with what is known of Herod. The story is a warning of what will happen at the end of Jesus' life, when the authorities will again seek to kill him.

Notice, finally, how Matthew sees scripture fulfilled in Jesus' flight to Egypt (2.15) and childhood in Nazareth (2.23). Once again, however, his use of scripture strikes us as artificial, though his method of finding hidden meanings in Old Testament texts was in keeping with the Jewish approach to scripture at that time. The passage in Hos. 11.1 originally referred to Israel. As for that quoted in 2.23, no such passage is known! Possibly Matthew is quoting an unusual version of a text which we do not recognize.

By the time that Matthew takes up the story at the place where Mark chose to begin, we already know a great deal about Jesus. Like Mark, he has made quite sure that we understand the full significance of the story which we are about to read.

Luke: *1–2*

Like Matthew, Luke has chosen to begin his story with so-called 'infancy narratives'. But again like Matthew, Luke tells these stories, not as a modern biographer would, out of straightforward interest in his subject's childhood, but because they seem to him to convey vital theological information.

We have seen that Matthew is concerned to show how Jesus fulfilled scripture. He does this by pointing out that the events he describes were the fulfilment of certain Old Testament quotations. Luke has the same concern, but he does things rather differently. Instead of quoting particular texts, he uses words and phrases which continually remind one of the Old Testament. He seems to have soaked himself in the Greek version of the Old Testament, and deliberately to have used its language and style. In this way, he was able to convey to his first readers the feeling that what they read was the continuation of the Old Testament story: God was continuing to act—in Jesus, and in the life of the Church, just as he had acted in the past. Notice especially how some of the 'hymns' in Lk. *1–2* (*1*.14–17, 32–5, 46–55, 68–79; 2.14, 29–32, 34 f.) remind one of the language of the Psalms.

Luke was a literary man, and he introduced his work with a formal literary opening (*1*.1–4). Like Mark, he chose to begin his account of the gospel with John the Baptist, but he took his story back to the birth of John. We have already seen that Mark was interested in John because he was the forerunner of Jesus, and the same is true of Luke. Notice how the stories of John and Jesus are told alternately. We have first of all the story of Gabriel announcing John's coming birth to Zechariah, who refuses to believe his message (*1*.5–25). This is followed by the familiar story of the annunciation by Gabriel—of Jesus' birth to Mary, who accepts the angel's word (*1*.26–38). Then the two mothers meet—and the unborn John recognizes the coming Messiah (*1*.39–56).

Next we have the account of the birth and naming of John (*1*.57–66). His father Zechariah finds his tongue, and bursts into song—a parallel to Mary's song in *1*.46–55. Notice how this song (the Benedictus) is really about Jesus, not John, until we come to vv. 76 ff. But Luke has not mixed up the babies! The point is that John's birth—like his mission—is a sign pointing forward to the one who follows him.

So we come to the birth of Jesus, and Luke tells of the journey to Bethlehem, the city of David (*2*.1–7); perhaps Luke saw the lack of a proper bed as a symbol of Jesus' homelessness (cf. Lk. *9*.58). In this gospel, Jesus is visited by humble shepherds instead of wise men (*2*.8–20). Luke then tells us how Jesus' parents fulfilled the regulations of the Law (*2*.21–4) and how Jesus was recognized in the Temple by Simeon and Anna, who both prophesied about his mission (*2*.25–38). Finally, we have a section about Jesus' childhood (*2*.39–52; cf. the reference to John's childhood in *1*.80) including the story of Jesus in the Temple, engaged in discussion with the religious teachers—another sign of what is to come.

Once again, by the time we get to the point where Mark began his story, we already know most of the things about Jesus which Mark set out in his opening paragraphs. We know, e.g., that John is to be the forerunner of Jesus, who is to be the Messiah, the successor of David (*1*.32–69); and we know that Jesus will be known as Son of God (*1*.32, 35); we are told that God took pleasure in him (*2*.40, 52); we know that the Holy Spirit is at work in both John and Jesus from the beginning (*1*.15 and 34). Notice the way in which much of this information is given to us in the words attributed to the angels and to various people (Zechariah, Mary, Simeon) who prophesy in the power of the Spirit. It is easy to pick out these passages in a modern translation, because they are printed in the form of verse. These 'hymns' are packed with theological information. The angels and inspired singers of songs in these first two chapters of Luke serve the same kind of function as the Chorus in a Greek play, who chime in every now and then to comment on the significance of what is taking place on the stage.

The Johannine Prologue: *1*.1–18

Let us turn finally to John, and see how he chose to begin his gospel. We realize immediately that we are in a totally different atmosphere. Like Matthew and Luke, John decided to begin his story before the arrival of John the Baptist at the River Jordan. Instead of beginning with the birth of Jesus, however, he goes back to the creation of the world. His opening words 'In the beginning' echo the opening words of Genesis. Like the other evangelists, John wants us to understand that what is happening in Jesus is the work of God, the continuation of his activity in the past. So he uses the idea of the Logos, or Word of God. The 'Word' is something much more active and powerful than a mere part of speech: for God, to speak is to act (cf. Isa. *55*.11). John believes that God has 'spoken' in the creation ' "Let there be light"; and there was light' (Gn. *1*.3); in the Law which he gave to Moses on

19

Sinai; in the words which he put into the mouths of the prophets. In all these ways he has acted in the past, and revealed his character to his people. But now he has acted and spoken in a new and more intimate way, for 'the Word became flesh, and dwelt among us' (*1*.14).

For the Jews, the clearest expression of God's word was to be found in the Torah—the Law given to Israel through Moses on Sinai. John, of course, like the other evangelists, believed that the teaching and activity of Jesus were 'in accordance with the scriptures'; Jesus was, as it were, in the succession—there was no discontinuity between God's activity in the past and his self-revelation in Christ. But clearly John is concerned to stress also that Jesus is superior to everything before him—superior even to that self-revelation of God on Sinai. So he stresses the contrast between Jesus and Moses. The Law was given to Moses; but grace and truth (the characteristics of God himself) have come in Jesus Christ. In him we have seen the glory of God (a glory which Moses only glimpsed on Sinai). God has been made known to us now through his only Son.

After the simple yet dramatic language of these opening verses (Jn. *1*.1–18, often referred to as the Prologue of the gospel), we come down to earth with John's version of the story of John the Baptist in vv. 19 ff. Once again, however, the evangelist has supplied us with vital theological information, which will help us to understand the story which follows.

After looking at the very different ways in which the evangelists begin their gospels, it is clear that they have at least one thing in common. Each of them offers us his interpretation of the story of Jesus. Each of them, after all, is writing 'gospel', good news, not an 'objective' account of what happened (if such a thing were possible!). All of them tell the story of Jesus in the light of later events—and what he said and did looked totally different in the light of the resurrection. We have seen how the resurrection is central in the earliest declarations of faith that we have. The gospels are written by those who believe in Jesus as the Risen Lord, and who wish to share that faith with others. Their purpose in writing is, indeed, stated quite clearly at the end of John's gospel:

These things are written that you may believe that Jesus is the Christ, the Son of God, and that believing you may have life in his name (Jn. 20.31).

Sometimes Christians are disturbed, when they come to study the gospels seriously, by the discovery that they do not offer us the 'objective facts' of the ministry of Jesus. It is perhaps surprising that anyone expects to find this sort of information in the gospels: a moment's reflection on the very different accounts which are given of any one event in the daily newspapers should make one realize that it is impossible ever to separate 'fact' from interpretation! We all see things from our own standpoint, and inevitably interpret any event in the light of our own knowledge, upbringing, understanding and prejudices. If Christians continue to expect something different in the gospels, it is perhaps because they have clung to the idea that 'gospel truth' is somehow different. Possibly the idea that the gospels were inspired has suggested the notion that their contents were dictated by the Holy Spirit, rather than being written by men subject to ordinary human limitations. Preachers have often been reluctant, in their exposition of scripture, to acknowledge that interpretation is 'built-in' to the stories in the gospels. Of course when we read these stories we interpret them from our own point of view; we relate them to our own experiences. But we need to remember that what we read has already been interpreted by those who told and retold the stories in the past: they were told precisely because they were relevant to the needs and experience of those who read them.

Christians ought not to be dismayed by this. We cannot have 'pure facts' and we should never have expected them. What we have is something far more exciting: different accounts of the ways in which early Christians understood their faith in Jesus and expressed their beliefs. And though we will often want to express our faith in ways which are different again, the preacher at least should be grateful to discover that the evangelists have offered him some useful leads in tackling the question 'What does this mean for me?'

Note: We have used the traditional names for the authors of the evangelists throughout this chapter because this is convenient, though their identity is, as we shall see, uncertain.
Read *Groundwork* 12b, 15 and 28.

Suggestions for further reading

* T. G. A. Baker, *What is the New Testament?* (SCM).
Brian E. Beck, *Reading the New Testament Today* (Lutterworth).

Chapter 2

'Who then is this?'—St. Mark I

Mark *1*.14–*8*.30.

MARK'S gospel is the shortest of the four, and almost certainly the earliest. It was Mark, apparently, who invented the new literary form of a 'gospel'. In many ways, however, he was not a literary man. His style is anything but polished, and he tends to use two words where one would do, and to join his stories together in the simplest of ways. Notice how often he uses the word 'and', and the phrase 'and immediately'. It looks as if, much of the time, Mark simply wrote down the stories as they came to him. His arrangement of the material, however—the *order* in which he places his stories—is more sophisticated: he has a message to get across, and he makes sure that his readers grasp it.

It is a good idea to begin studying Mark by reading through the gospel itself, before looking at the notes given here or at any commentaries. Read through Mark *1*.14–*8*.30, making your own outline of the book. Try to forget all the sermons you have heard—and preached—on this gospel, and to read it as though you were reading it for the first time. What kind of impact does Mark's account make? What sort of stories does he use? What themes does he emphasize? What impression does he give of Jesus? Then read through this half of the gospel again with the aid of the notes which follow, and see if your own analysis agrees with the one given here.

Jesus claims authority

1.14–15. *Jesus proclaims the Kingdom.* The first thing which Jesus did, according to Mark, was to announce that the time of fulfilment had arrived: God's Kingdom was at hand. According to the dictionary, the word 'kingdom' means 'territory under the rule of a king'. In this case, of course, the 'territory' is the world, which has fallen into enemy hands; men and demonic powers have usurped the throne. But now the time is at hand when God is going to restore his rule, and that means the punishment of the wicked, as well as salvation for those who have been faithful to him. It is a time of judgment—which means that there is need to repent, even though Jesus' message is 'good news'.

1.16–20. *Jesus calls four disciples.* Mark's gospel is a story about discipleship, and this account of the call of the fishermen comes at the very beginning of the story. Mark does not tell us whether they had already met Jesus or heard him preach; possibly they had. What interests Mark is the authority of Jesus: he calls them to follow him, and immediately they leave their nets and follow. This simple story of the immediate response to Jesus made by these four men presents us with a vivid picture of the personal impact made by Jesus.

1.21–2. *Jesus teaches with authority.* Worship in the synagogue consisted of prayers, readings from the Law and Prophets, and expositions of the readings. Its conduct was not in the hands of the priests, who were concerned only with worship in the Temple at Jerusalem, but was the responsibility of the local elders. Any man who was competent to do so could contribute to the exposition of scripture on the invitation of the synagogue ruler. This is what Jesus does here—but the congregation is astonished at his teaching, because he teaches with authority.

1.23–8. *Jesus' authority over unclean spirits.* Belief in demons was widespread in Judaism at this time, and many illnesses

24

were attributed to demon-possession. Here we have the first of several exorcisms recorded in the gospel. The unclean spirit, speaking through the mouth of its unfortunate victim, not only recognizes who Jesus is—'the Holy One of God' (v. 24)—but realizes that his coming means the destruction of evil. Jesus silences the spirit, though in fact its words are not heard—or at least are not fully understood—by those present; once again it is only we, the readers, who understand the significance of what is happening. The crowd in the synagogue merely marvel at the authority with which Jesus is able to command even unclean spirits.

1.29–32. Jesus heals a friend. In the synagogue, Jesus expelled the demon with one authoritative command; now, he heals a sick woman with a touch. The result is equally dramatic, and the woman's cure is shown in the fact that she is able to serve her guests.

1.32–5. Healings and exorcisms. After sunset, when the sabbath had ended, the whole city flocked to Jesus. This simple summary leaves us in no doubt about Jesus' authority to heal the sick and cast out demons.

1.5–9. Jesus extends his ministry. Jesus escapes from Capernaum in order to pray, and decides that he must move on to other towns, in order to preach there. We are not meant to think of his role as preacher being in conflict with his role as healer; the two belong together, as we shall see. But he cannot confine his ministry to one city. 'For that is why I came out' probably means 'that is why I left home'—i.e., to preach throughout the whole region. And this is what he now does (v. 39).

1.40–5. Jesus makes a leper clean. We cannot be sure that the man described here as a 'leper' was suffering from the disease which we know as leprosy. Until very recently, leprosy was incurable, but there are provisions in Lev. *13* and *14* for the 'cleansing' of a leper, so that the term must have been used for victims of other skin complaints besides leprosy, some of which were self-limiting. Whatever the exact nature of his disease, the 'leper' was doubly unfortunate, since he was not allowed to mix with his fellows, and so was exiled from society; he was as good as dead. The leper here takes a risk, in daring to approach Jesus. At this point there is an important variant in our manuscripts. According to some of them, Mark tells us that Jesus was angry—a statement so surprising that we can understand why, at a very early stage, a scribe might substitute the word 'compassion' for 'anger', and why many others followed suit. Although many translators have accepted this reading, it seems much more probable that Mark described Jesus as angry. The problem is to know why. It seems unlikely that he thought of Jesus as being angry with the leper, more likely that he thought of him as angry with Satan as the cause of the man's suffering. Jesus then 'stretched out his hand and touched him'—a normal action in healing, but on this occasion quite extraordinary, since in touching a leper, Jesus was making himself 'unclean' according to the Law. Such is his power, however, that instead of being made unclean, he is able to say to the leper 'Be clean'. In dramatic form, we see the authority of Jesus to provide remedies which the Law was unable to provide for those who were sick and outcasts from society. All the Law can do is provide the correct rituals when the man is restored to health. But Jesus does not attack the Law—he commands the man to fulfil it, so that he can mix in society again (v. 44). Jesus' power is greater than the Law, but it does not conflict with the Law; however, as the next few stories show, it conflicts with those who regard themselves as the upholders of the Law.

2.1–12. *Authority to forgive sins.* Here for the first time we meet the theme of conflict between Jesus and the religious authorities which plays such an important part in Mark's gospel. The story told here is of another healing, but it has an unusual twist to it, for in the middle we have a conversation between Jesus and the scribes which indicates the true significance of what is happening.

Jesus is back in Capernaum, 'at home'—perhaps in Peter's house. The crowd is such that in desperation the sick man's friends climbed the outside stair and dug through the roof. It would not have been too difficult to break up the mixture of twigs, matting and earth which was used to fill the space between the beams of the roof. Instead of the expected word of healing, Jesus says 'Your sins are forgiven'. Since popular opinion regarded physical misfortune as the result of sin (cf. Jn. 9.1–3), it may well be that this man needed to be assured of forgiveness before he could respond to a physical cure. Jesus does more, however, than assure the man that God has forgiven him; he himself assumes the authority to forgive—something which seems blasphemous to the scribes, the orthodox teachers of the Law. But though Jesus has claimed to exercise the authority which belongs to God alone, he now demonstrates that his claim is not an empty one by speaking the word of healing. As usual, the story ends with the amazement of the crowd at the extraordinary power of Jesus.

Jesus claims authority here as 'the Son of man'. We meet here for the first time an important phrase which is found repeatedly in the gospels in the mouth of Jesus. Unfortunately there is little agreement among scholars as to what it means. Traditionally it has been assumed that Jesus used the phrase as a mysterious way of referring to himself. It has been suggested that he avoided the term 'Christ', because it was open to misunderstanding, and adopted the title 'the Son of man' instead. If so, however, it seems that this term was even more open to misunderstanding. In recent years, many scholars have come to believe that Jesus was not in fact referring to himself when he spoke of the Son of man, but to another figure, who was to come in the future in judgement. They have argued that first-century Jews were expecting this 'Son of man', and that it would therefore have been natural for Jesus to announce his coming. If some of the gospel sayings about the Son of man (like the one in 2.10) now clearly refer to Jesus, this is due, they say, to a misunderstanding on the part of the Church. Others have suggested that the phrase was nothing more, in the mouth of Jesus, than a somewhat elaborate way of saying 'I', and certainly it seems that the evangelists understood Jesus to be referring to himself, even if modern scholars have their doubts.

What we need to explain, however, is how it is that the term 'the Son of man' is used in such very different contexts: it is found in passages where Jesus claims unusual authority (2.10, 28), in references to future vindication (8.38, 13.26, 14.62), and declarations of the necessity for suffering and death (e.g. 8.31; 9.31; 10.33). To many of us, the best explanation seems to be that Jesus chose the term, not because it was a ready-made 'title', but because it seemed to him a suitable way of expressing the role which he felt called to fulfil. In other words, we should not suppose that the Jews were expecting the arrival of someone called 'the Son of man' and that Jesus was claiming to be this figure; rather that he used the phrase as a way of reminding the people of the mission of Israel described in Dan. 7. In the vision described there, the one like a Son of man is understood to be a symbol of the faithful remnant of Israel, at present suffering because of their obedience to God, but soon to be vindicated by God and given authority to rule over the earth in his name. If Jesus claimed authority as the Son of man, was it because he saw himself fulfilling the role of obedient Israel? Whatever the explanation for Jesus' own use of the term, Mark certainly believed it to be an appropriate one in referring to his authority.

2.13–17. *Jesus and the outcasts.* Here we have two short stories. First, the call of another disciple, and then the account of a meal. In both cases, Jesus is mixing with the outcasts of society. Either we may conclude that Jesus is no better than they, as the scribes do (v. 16), or we may see here another example of Jesus' authority in bringing men and women salvation, as does Mark (v. 17).

Levi's name does not appear in the list of twelve disciples given in Mk. 3.16–19. There is no difficulty about this, since the twelve are said to have been chosen from a wider number of disciples. However, in Matthew's gospel, the story is told of a tax-gatherer called Matthew—probably the result of a mix-up in names at some stage. As a tax-gatherer, employed by the Romans, Levi would be hated by his fellow countrymen and despised by the religious authorities for mixing with foreigners. For Jesus to call fishermen to be his disciples was extraordinary, but to call a tax-gatherer was scandalous! The story is a demonstration of the saving grace of God at work in Jesus. So, too, is the account of the meal which Jesus shares 'with tax collectors and sinners'. The scribes disapprove, not only because of the character of the company, but because it was unlikely that such people had bothered to carry out all the regulations about washing and preparing the food and dishes. They are outraged that Jesus should ignore these things. Jesus, however, is concerned with something more important than ritual cleanness; he is concerned to bring wholeness to those who know that they are sinners.

2.18–22. *Old and new.* Once again we have a passage which raises the question of Jesus' religious practice—or lack of it. Strict Jews fasted twice a week; the disciples of John the Baptist did the same. Why did Jesus' disciples fail to do so? His answer comes in the form of a parable: when a marriage celebration is going on, the guests do not fast, but feast! Verse 20 is strange—bridegrooms are not usually 'taken away'. Possibly this is a saying which has been added to the original parable. When we read vv. 19 and 20 together, it is clear that Mark understands the bridegroom to refer to Jesus himself. But taken on its own, v. 19 could mean simply that since Jesus brings good news of salvation, this is a time of rejoicing. Fasting belongs to the old era, not to the present.

The two sayings in vv. 21 and 22 also contrast the old and the new. What is happening in the ministry of Jesus is so new and vital that it marks a new beginning. By the time Mark wrote, the truth of this was probably apparent: Judaism was unable to contain the 'new wine' of Christianity.

2.23–8. *Lord of the sabbath.* Once again Jesus is challenged regarding the activity of his disciples. In plucking the ears of grain they were held to be breaking the Law, since reaping was said by the Pharisees to be one of the activities which was forbidden on the sabbath. Jesus replies by quoting the case of David (regarded as a model of piety) who ate the shewbread in the time of Abiathar (in fact it was when Abiathar's father,

Ahimelech, was high priest). The two cases are quite different, since David and his companions were hungry, and there is no such pressing need in the case of the disciples. The attitude of those Pharisees who hedged the Law around with countless prohibitions for fear of breaking its least regulation, should have led them, if they were logical, to condemn David also. In Jesus' eyes, they have got things back to front: 'the sabbath was made for man, not man for the sabbath'. They desire to do God's will, but their very eagerness to do so turns the sabbath, given to them as a privilege, into a burden. No doubt many Jewish rabbis would have agreed with Jesus, since sayings similar to v. 27 can be found in Jewish writings. The final saying, however, claims authority once again for Jesus, the Son of man, as lord of the sabbath.

3.1–6. The opposition hardens. Another story of conflict between Jesus and the religious authorities, once again on the subject of sabbath observance. This time it is Jesus himself who is accused of 'breaking' the sabbath. His question to the Pharisees sets out the point at issue between them and himself. Their attitude is negative: they think in terms of not doing things which they consider unlawful. His attitude is positive—as was demonstrated in the previous story. Had the man's life been in danger, the Pharisees would have permitted emergency treatment. Jesus refuses to draw a distinction between 'saving life' in the narrowest sense and offering wholeness of life to a sick man. The sabbath is meant for the glory of God and the benefit of man—why, then, should he not 'do good' and 'save life'? Notice how the opposition to Jesus has built up since the beginning of chapter 2; now the Pharisees are deliberately looking for an opportunity to attack Jesus (*3.2*). By the time we reach *3.6*, the end of the story is already inevitable. According to Mark, the Pharisees join with the supporters of Herod—an extraordinary combination of interests—in plotting to destroy a common enemy.

Miracles and parables demonstrate Jesus' authority

3.7–12. The crowds follow Jesus. The Jewish religious

authorities may have rejected Jesus, but the ordinary people respond to him; the crowd described here represents the whole nation. Many of them came for healing. As before, the unclean spirits are said to have recognized him, and to have acknowledged his authority over them.

3.13–19. The Twelve. The choice of twelve men was probably intended as symbolic: they represent the twelve tribes or patriarchs of Israel. They are appointed, first, 'to be with him', that is to be disciples, and secondly, 'to be sent out to preach and have authority to cast out demons', something which happens after *6.7.*

3.20–35. By whose power? We return once again to the theme of conflict between Jesus and the religious authorities, but now the question at issue is how Jesus is able to do the things which he does. Granted that he has the power to exorcize demons, who has given him this power? First of all, we have the answer of those who ought to have been most sympathetic to Jesus, his own family (v. 21; the RSV translates the Greek here as 'friends', but the NEB's 'family' is a more likely translation). They think that he is out of his mind—that is, that he is himself possessed by a demon. A similar answer is given by the scribes from Jerusalem—men of greater learning and authority than the local scribes we have met so far. According to them Jesus is possessed by Beelzebub or Beelzebul—another name for Satan, the prince of demons. In their view, Jesus is a law-breaker, and his teaching is contrary to the revealed will of God. If he possesses supernatural power, it must be because he is in league with the devil. Jesus replies again in parables—two short sayings, in vv. 24–5, which show the absurdity of this accusation. This is not a case of civil war in Satan's kingdom! The true explanation comes in another parable in v. 27: Satan's kingdom is being plundered because his territory has been invaded, and he has been defeated.

The saying in vv. 28–9 shows us the seriousness of the scribes' accusation. What they have done is to attribute the activity of the Holy Spirit to Satan. The 'unforgiveable sin' is

31

the deliberate refusal to acknowledge the work of the Holy Spirit, the attitude which calls goodness evil and truth false. These men are 'guilty of an eternal sin' because they are so obstinate that they cannot change. Notice the irony of the situation: the religious leaders, the guardians of the Law, are themselves found guilty of this, the greatest sin, at the very moment when they think they are doing their religious duty.

The family of Jesus now return to the scene. Jesus' reaction to them seems harsh: his true kinsmen are not those who are related to him by blood, but those who do the will of God (vv. 33 f). The point of the story, however, is not that Jesus has rejected his family, but they have rejected him. In v. 21, Mark told us that they thought Jesus mad. Now they stand 'outside' and send for Jesus, in contrast to those who sit 'about him' (vv. 31 f.). This is why Jesus points to those who are prepared to listen to him and follow him, and describes them as his true family.

Notice the way in which Mark has woven his material together here, so that we get one story (that of the scribes) inside another (that of Jesus' family). This 'sandwich' form is typical of Mark. He uses it here in order to draw a parallel between the attitude of Jesus' own family and that of the religious authorities. Both groups have failed to recognize and accept the authority of Jesus. In the course of Mark's story, other groups will follow their example, until Jesus is totally rejected by his people.

Christian tradition has assumed that Mary was sympathetic towards Jesus' ministry. In fact we know nothing about her attitude at this time. Mark's account here suggests that both she and Jesus' brothers were opposed to him. But this may be Mark's own interpretation of the tradition, since he may well have brought together three stories which had once circulated independently (v. 21, vv. 22 ff., vv. 31–5).

4.1–20. The parable of the sower. Mark has several times told us that Jesus taught. Now at last he sets out some of that teaching, and he begins with the parable of the sower. The story is simple, yet dramatically told: we hear first of one

failure, then of another, then of a third, and finally of the
seed which germinated and grew successfully. But what does
it mean? Mark supplies us with an explanation in vv. 13–20.
'Do you not understand this parable?' asks Jesus. 'How then
are you to understand any parable?' This is a parable about
parables! It is meant to be the key to all the rest. The sower is
Jesus, and he sows the word of the gospel. Many of those
who hear Jesus fail to respond to him (v. 15); others welcome his message, but for various reasons their response
proves shortlived (vv. 17, 19). Others, however, hear Jesus'
message and accept it, and in them the seed bears fruit. Most
commentators believe that this explanation of the parable
originated in the early Christian community, rather than
with Jesus himself: the reference to persecution in v. 17, e.g.,
suggests the kind of thing which his followers had to face at
the time when Mark was writing. In other words, vv. 14–20
are an early 'sermon', drawing out the meaning of Jesus'
parable. It is unlikely, in fact, that Jesus needed to explain
his parables. The word 'parable' can mean 'riddle', and
clearly by the time Mark came to write his gospel, he found
many of the parables very puzzling. A story which is told in
one setting (to a group of people facing particular circumstances) can be totally meaningless when it is told in another.
This is why Mark has 'sandwiched' together the parable of
the sower and its explanation with the difficult saying in
vv. 11–12, which seems to suggest that parables are meant to
hide the truth of the gospel from 'outsiders'. Mark knew that
many of the parables were very difficult to understand; they
needed to be explained. He also knew that most of those
who had heard Jesus teaching had rejected that teaching.
Equally puzzling was the fact that the great majority of Jews
continued to reject the Christian gospel. What had happened to God's purpose of salvation for his people? Strange
as it seemed, their refusal to respond must be part of God's
plan. So Mark concluded that the divine purpose was to
conceal the truth about Jesus from the great majority of men
and women, and that Jesus himself had intended his teaching
to be obscure.

In their original context, however, the parables were

intended to help men and women see the truth, not to confuse them. The Greek word for 'parable' means, literally, 'put alongside'. Put one of these stories alongside one's own situation, and it's a case of 'if the cap fits, wear it'. That is precisely what happened in the case of David, confronted by Nathan's parable in 2 Sam. *12*.1–7. Sometimes we see it happening in the gospels, e.g. Mark *12*.12. But often what happens in the gospels is that we have parables which have been told and retold, applied and reapplied to changing situations, as the Church heard the words of Jesus addressing them. When we come to study Matthew and Luke, we shall look at some examples of the way in which some of the parables have been adapted in order to bring out the relevance of their message to new situations.

Mark has misunderstood the purpose of the parables. But he was surely right when he interpreted the parable of the sower as a parable about the response which men and women make to the teaching of Jesus. The parable speaks of four groups but that is part of the story-teller's art: certainly as Mark understood it, there are really only two groups—those who respond to Jesus and those who do not. Those who do not respond are those 'outside', whose hearts have been hardened; those who respond, who hear and follow Jesus, are those to whom the secret of the Kingdom is given (vv. 11–12). Although Jesus does not preach himself, or announce himself as God's Messiah, the effect of his teaching, as it is presented to us by Mark, is to confront us with a decision about Jesus. Either we accept his teaching or we reject it: whichever we do, we accept or reject not only his teaching, but Jesus himself, and the Kingdom which he proclaims.

4.21–5. *Sayings on the same theme*. We have here a collection of sayings which probably did not originally belong together, for we find them scattered throughout both Matthew and Luke. Mark placed them here because they seemed to him to continue the theme of the previous section. The saying in v. 21 seems in fact to contradict his understanding of parables. Of course one does not hide a lamp under a meal-tub! Of course the good news brought by Jesus is not meant to be hidden. But the next saying shows us how Mark has interpreted v. 21. What was hidden during the ministry of Jesus is going to be revealed later; what was obscure then will eventually be made plain.

Verses 24–5 are a warning. Mark probably regarded them as summing up the message of vv. 1–20: those who accept Jesus' words will be given the joys of God's kingdom, but those who reject them will lose even the opportunity to hear the gospel which was once given them.

4.26–34. Two parables about the kingdom. These two parables, unlike that of the sower, are specifically said to be about the kingdom of God. In both of them, the point of the parable is the contrast between the tiny seed and the large crop or shrub which grows from it. These parables have been interpreted in many ways. Some have argued that the 'seed' was sown in the past, in the time of the prophets, and Jesus' ministry is to be understood as the time of harvest. Others argue that the seed is sown by Jesus, and the harvest belongs to the end of history. Some think the parables urge patience, because God's kingdom comes so slowly; in fact, the mustard plant is very fast-growing. Jesus may have used these parables to assure his hearers that God's kingdom would come, even though they could not see it yet. For Mark, they illustrate the principle set out in v. 22. The kingdom of God is already present in the ministry of Jesus, but it is like seed thrown on to the earth: unless you are let into the secret, you do not know it is there. But what the kingdom will finally be is a very different matter.

4.35–41. Authority over wind and waves. Following the section of parables, we have a group of four miracle stories. The story of the stilling of the storm is the first of the so-called 'nature miracles', but for Mark its significance is similar to the previous miracles: it demonstrates the authority of Jesus—this time over wind and waves. It is impossible now for the historian to answer the question 'What happened?' Whatever explanation we may give for the story, its importance lies in the fact that it shows us that the early followers of

Jesus were convinced that he had acted with the power of God himself.

The Sea of Galilee is subject, because of its position, to storms which begin and end abruptly. The disciples address Jesus as 'Teacher' (or 'rabbi'), and their words are rough and indignant. Jesus rebukes the wind and sea, very much as he rebukes unclean spirits: storms were thought to be caused by rebellious spiritual powers. Jesus rebukes the disciples for their lack of faith: their fear shows their failure to trust God. Their reaction to the power of Jesus, however, is to be even more afraid: confronted with such authority, they are awestruck. It is God who at the creation brought order out of the watery chaos (Gn. *1*), and God alone who controls the raging of the sea (Ps. *89*.8 f). 'Who then is this, that even wind and sea obey him?'

*5.*1–20. *Authority over demons.* This story forms a pair with the previous one: Jesus is able to control not only the raging of wind and waves but the raging of a man possessed by demons. The man lives among tombs—the haunt of demons, and regarded as an 'unclean' place. Verses 3–4 describe the man's enormous strength, but in Jesus he meets one who is stronger, who has already bound Satan himself (*3.*27). Like others possessed by spirits he recognizes Jesus, and flings himself at his feet (vv. 6 f.). This man believes himself to be possessed by a large number of demons. Pigs are regarded by Jews as unclean animals, so this is presumably Gentile territory. It was appropriate that unclean spirits should live in unclean animals, but the pigs immediately rush into the sea and are drowned, presumably destroying the demons also. Jesus has not only rescued the man from their power, but has destroyed the demons as well. Modern readers tend to be worried by the idea that Jesus permitted the destruction of innocent animals, but Mark was not worried about the pigs—they were unclean, like the demons, and their destruction only proper. The reaction of those who witnessed the miracle, and those who observed the dramatic change in the demoniac, is the usual one: fear (vv. 14–15). The man wants to follow Jesus, but he is told to go and take the good news of what has happened to him to his family and friends. He is to tell them what the Lord (i.e. God) has done for him. Mark tells us that the man went off and proclaimed what Jesus had done for him—so reminding us that in the activity of Jesus we are to see the activity of God himself. There is no suggestion here, as on some occasions, that the cure should be kept secret. The Decapolis was predominately Gentile: though Jesus did not preach in Gentile territory, he commanded that God's activity and mercy should be preached there.

5.21–43. *Power to restore life.* Mark's second pair of miracle stories in this section are told together, one of them forming an interlude (vv. 25–34) within the other. There is an obvious link between the two stories. Jesus restores life, not only to the twelve-year-old child, but to the woman from whom strength has been draining away for twelve years. Jesus is now shown as one who has authority over life itself. The child is at the point of death, beyond all normal human aid (v. 23). The woman, also, has exhausted human skill. Her affliction is not only physical, however; like the leper in *1*.40 ff., she is an outcast from society because her illness makes her ritually unclean (Lev. *15*.25–30). It is for this reason, not simply out of modesty, that she approaches Jesus secretly. Both Jesus and the woman know immediately that power has passed from one to the other. Like others who have experienced the amazing power of Jesus, she is overcome with fear and trembling. Yet she at least has shown faith, and it is this which has saved her.

One interesting feature of the story about the dead child is that much of the vocabulary used would be appropriate in preaching about the Christian hope of resurrection: the verbs 'to save' (RSV 'to make well') and 'to live' (v. 23), the contrast between death and sleep (v. 39), the mockery of the bystanders (v. 40), and the statement that the child rose up (v. 42, RSV 'got up'), all suggest that those who heard the story might see in it another significance. (Cf. the way in which the story of Lazarus is interpreted in John *11*).

Jesus' command to tell no one what has happened (v. 43) seems absurd. It seems especially strange after the story of the sick woman, who was not allowed to keep her cure a secret from the crowd. But just as it was important for the woman to acknowledge her faith in Jesus, and not treat him simply as as worker of magic, so it is important for the family of the child not to babble about Jesus' ability to raise the dead. These things need to be seen and to be spoken about in the context of faith in Jesus: the miracles are not simply 'wonders', but signs of the kingdom of God which Jesus proclaims.

In both these stories, Jesus has come into contact with those who were, in Jewish eyes, 'unclean'. But instead of being made unclean himself, his power has restored them both to wholeness.

6.1–6. *Disbelief at home.* In contrast to the faith (however inadequate) of those who come to Jesus for help, we have a story of the failure of those in his home town to believe in him. Like others who have heard Jesus teach, they are astonished at his wisdom and authority, but astonishment soon turns to disbelief. Mark is not afraid to say that Jesus could not do any mighty works there (notice how Matthew tones this down, Matt. *13*.58). It is not simply that Jesus refuses to perform miracles; rather, it is that they cannot be done except in a context of faith—and this faith (with a few exceptions) is lacking. The mighty works of Jesus are signs of God's kingdom, and go hand in hand with its proclamation.

The twelve: hard hearts and the dawn of understanding

6.7–13. *Jesus sends out the twelve.* The twelve were sent out to preach repentance, and with authority over unclean spirits. In other words, they were sent out to share in Jesus' own mission to Israel. Their task was an urgent one, so they were to travel light. The details of what the disciples should and should not take with them differ in the three synoptic gospels, because the accounts have been adapted to suit local conditions: shoes, e.g., might be essential on some journies, unnecessary on others. If the disciples were welcomed, they were to accept the hospitality offered them; if they were not received, they were to shake the dust of the place from their feet as a sign that those who had rejected their message were themselves rejected and no longer true members of Israel. Any Jew returning to Israel from abroad shook the dust off his feet in order not to contaminate Jewish soil.

6.14–29. The death of John the Baptist. Between the sending out of the twelve and their return, Mark inserts the story of the death of John the Baptist. There seems to be no logical connexion between the two stories, but the interruption creates the impression of the passing of time, and perhaps this is Mark's intention.

Verses 14–15 raise again the question 'Who is Jesus?' The popular answers are that he is Elijah, a prophet, or John the Baptist restored to life. The story about John which follows is the only one in the gospel which is not specifically about Jesus. Yet even this, we may guess, has been included by Mark because it has something to tell us about Jesus. Just as John was the forerunner of Jesus in his work of baptism and preaching (*1*.1–8), so now he is his forerunner in death (see *9*.12 f.): if the messenger is rejected, the one who follows will be rejected too.

6.30–1. Return of the twelve. Mark refers to the twelve here as 'apostles'. The Greek word represents a Hebrew term, *shaliah*, meaning someone who is authorized to act as one's representative on a particular mission. This was precisely the function of the twelve on this occasion, but of course by the time Mark wrote his gospel the word had become a technical term in the Christian community.

6.32–45. Five thousand fed. This is the only miracle story recorded by all four evangelists, which suggests that it played an important role in early Christian circles. Many attempts have been made to answer the question 'What happened?', but unfortunately this cannot be done. Suggestions that the numbers have been exaggerated, or that the feeding was only a symbolic one, or that the people were persuaded to share food they had brought with them, cannot explain the belief of all the evangelists that this was a miraculous event. Whatever happened, the significance of the story for them was that it presented, in dramatic form, a further truth about Jesus. The belief that Jesus fed the people was interpreted by them in relation to their belief that God had fed his people with manna in the wilderness (Ex. *16;* Num. *11*). The Jewish hope was that in the coming messianic age, God would once again give the people manna. If Jesus now feeds the people in a desert place (vv. 31, 32, 35, translated 'lonely place' in RSV and NEB), it is a sign that the new age is dawning, and that Jesus is greater than Moses, who went before him. Jesus describes the people as being 'like sheep without a shepherd' (cf. Num. *27*.17; 1 Kgs. *22*.17; Ezek. *34*.5), and has compassion on them: their primary need is for teaching, because their leaders have failed them.

Jesus' actions are described in language similar to that used in *14*.22: 'taking' bread, he 'blessed, and broke . . . and gave' it to the disciples (v. 41). These were the natural actions for the head of the household to perform, but would surely remind Mark's readers of the eucharist, the meal which they ate together, at which Jesus was still host. This link is underlined by John in his account of the miracle (Jn. *6*).

But the crowd needed physical, as well as spiritual, food. Mark underlines the miraculous character of the incident: all the people were fully satisfied, and there were basketfuls of food left over (vv. 42–3).

6.45–52. *Jesus walks on water.* This short story bristles with difficulties for the modern reader. First of all, it appears to contradict scientific principles: men do not walk on water. This points us to a second, doctrinal difficulty: other miracles depict Jesus as possessing a more-than-human power, but this one, though demonstrating his superhuman gifts, is in danger of presenting him as less than fully human—only seeming to be like other men. Thirdly, while other miracles demonstrate the power of Jesus helping those in need, this one by comparison is 'useless'; the disciples are not in danger, and Jesus' appearance to them is really an 'epiphany'—a demonstration of his power—rather than an act of salvation. Here, however, we have the clue to Mark's use of the story. For him, the significance of the miracle is that it reveals Jesus' true nature. Only God is able to control the sea and to walk on the waves (Job 9.8); it was God who made his path through the sea at the Exodus, when he brought his people across the water (Ps. 77.19 f.; Isa. 43.16). Now Jesus comes to his disciples, walking across the sea. Mark comments that they were dumbfounded, because they had not understood the miracle of the loaves. Why does Mark link these two miracles together? (John does the same.) Perhaps because the crossing of the sea and the gift of manna are the two central miracles in the story of the Exodus. If the disciples had understood how Jesus could feed the people, they would not have been surprised to find him crossing the sea. But their hearts were hardened—like those of the Pharisees (3.5).

6.53–6. *Many healed.* This short summary was probably written by Mark himself. He means us to realize that the healings he had described in detail are typical of what happened again and again.

7.1–23. *A dispute about defilement.* Mark returns to the theme of official Judaism's disapproval of Jesus. The teaching given here is probably a collection of sayings: notice the repeated introductory phrases in vv. 6, 9, 14, 18 and 20.

In vv. 6–13, Jesus answers the complaints of the Pharisees by means of a counter-attack: their criticism of the disciples' behaviour is not based upon the Law itself, but on the Pharisees' own traditions about how the Law is to be understood. Jesus argues that in concentrating on the latter they have fallen into the danger of ignoring the former! They have kept the tradition of the elders—which hedged the Law about with countless regulations—and in doing so they have lost sight of the spirit of the Law. The rules about washing are based on ideas about ritual cleanliness—about what is holy, and what is 'common'—rather than what we would term clean and dirty. The first of these two sayings (vv. 6–8) is based on scripture, the second on a specific example of the way in which legalism could defeat the purpose of the Law.

The remaining sayings are also concerned with eating and

41

defilement, but now the issue is the food which is eaten, not the washing of hands. Jesus' teaching here seems at first sight to attack the Law itself, since according to Lev. *11* certain types of food did defile those who ate them. It is possible that when he says 'not this but that' we should understand this as an emphatic way of saying that one thing is more important than another: what *really* defiles a man is not this but that. In other words, the scribes are so busy worrying about ritual cleanliness that they are forgetting altogether about the more important matter of moral cleanliness. Nevertheless, the saying is important because it challenges the idea that God's will must be understood in terms of inflexible rules. Mark, however, seems to understand it in an even more radical way: Jesus is challenging the teaching of Lev. *11* itself—hence his explanatory comment in v. 19. Once again, Jesus is 'teaching with authority'—an authority much greater than that of the scribes, who debate the meaning of the Law, since he challenges the authority of the Law itself.

7.24–30. *A Gentile child healed.* This is the only occasion in Mark when he tells us that someone healed by Jesus was a Gentile. The story surprises us, because of Jesus' almost churlish reluctance to heal the sick child. We tend to assume that Jesus must have helped everyone who came to him, and that he included Gentiles in his ministry. In fact, the evidence suggests that he confined his attention to the Jews, and under-stood his mission as being to his own people. Since Mark has constantly emphasized that the miracles are closely linked with his preaching, and are to be seen as part of the breaking-in of God's kingdom, we ought not to be surprised if the idea of healing a Gentile is seen as an anomaly. The healing miracles take place only where there is faith. This Gentile woman requests a cure outside the context of Jesus' call to Israel; perhaps she regards him as a miracle-worker, and is simply taking advantage of his presence in the town. Jesus' reply suggests that his power to heal must not be treated in that way, since it belongs to something greater. The woman's reply is not simply a witty retort: she acknowledges that salvation belongs to Israel, and shows her faith in something greater than a wonder-worker's power to heal the sick. The placing of this story after 7.1–23 is significant. Christians arguing about whether or not Gentiles were to be admitted to the Church, and whether or not they must keep the Jewish food regulations, would have found both these sections relevant.

7.31–7. A deaf man hears. This is the first time Mark has described the cure of a deaf man. The theme of 'hearing' is, however, an important one in the gospel. Jesus has taught the crowds, continually urging them to listen, and to take care how they hear; so far, even the disciples have failed to understand what they have heard. Now a man without hearing is enabled to hear—and so to speak of what he has heard.

8.1–10. Four thousand fed. This story is basically the same as that told in *6.32–44*, but the details are different. This suggests that we have here a different tradition of the same event. Why did Mark include two such similar stories? Many commentators have argued that he meant us to understand the crowd in ch. *6* to have been Jewish, and that in ch. *8* to have been made up of Gentiles. But attempts to prove this by finding hidden meanings in the numbers given in this version of the story are unconvincing. If this was Mark's intention, he certainly has not made his point clear. In fact, he gives no indication of a ministry by Jesus to Gentiles. It is better to suppose that Mark included both stories because he believed that the power of Jesus to feed the people was especially significant.

The disciples' question in v. *4* seems extraordinarily foolish, following after the story of the earlier miracle. Mark did of course regard them as foolish, unable to see the truth which was, with the gift of hindsight, so obvious to him. When the story circulated on its own, however, the disciples' reaction would have seemed entirely normal.

Jesus' actions are described in the same language as before. The one significant difference is that this time he is said to have 'given thanks'. The Greek word used here is the one which has given us the term 'eucharist'.

8.11–13. Pharisees demand a sign. If the disciples seem foolish, how much more so the Pharisees when they come to Jesus and demand a sign! By placing this story immediately after the miracle of the feeding, Mark has emphasized the blindness of the Jewish authorities. They are unable to comprehend what is happening in front of their eyes. Of course Jesus will not perform a sign to order. The signs are clearly there, in the miracles, for those who have eyes to see, just as the secret of the kingdom is plainly given, in the parables, for those who have ears to hear (*4.*11 f.).

8.14–21. The disciples fail to understand. If the disciples here find it difficult to understand Jesus, commentators find it equally difficult to understand Mark. This is a very strange conversation. The main theme, however, is clearly the continuing failure to understand the significance of the miracles: after seeing Jesus provide bread for thousands on two occasions, they are still worried about having brought only one loaf with them! If they had understood these miracles, they would have realized that Jesus' power is all-sufficient: he is even greater than Moses, through whom God fed his people with manna.

But why does Jesus warn the disciples to beware of the leaven of the Pharisees and the Herodians (v. 15)? Perhaps Mark is thinking here of the hardness of heart shown by these groups, and the attitude which made them unable to recognize the significance of what Jesus was doing: the disciples were in the same danger. Luke uses this saying in another context, and interprets it of hypocrisy (Lk. *12.*1).

8.22–6. A blind man sees. After two stories about people who cannot see the obvious, we have a story about a blind man who gains his sight. Immediately following this, comes the story of how the disciples' eyes are opened—at least in part—to the truth about Jesus. It seems clear that Mark has deliberately put these stories together: for him, physical blindness is a symbol of the failure to understand who Jesus is. We need to read the stories one after another to see the way in which Mark interprets them. It is interesting to compare the different way in which the Fourth gospel makes the same kind of point. There too, in ch. 9, we find a story of a blind man who is given his sight; there too, the miracle is interpreted as a symbol of the way in which the blind man's eyes are opened to the truth of who Jesus is. But John makes quite sure that we understand this by weaving the two stories together. Mark is content to put his stories side by side, and he leaves us to see the connection.

This story is unusual, in that the man's cure is said to have taken place in two stages; perhaps it was thought to be particularly difficult. As a symbol of the disciples' growing understanding, Mark probably means us to think of this first stage as a parallel to the way in which even after Caesarea Philippi, they comprehend only half the truth. It is not until after the resurrection that they really understand.

8.27–30. The disciples' eyes are opened. Here we have the climax of this section of the gospel: the disciples, constantly rebuked for their lack of faith, at last find some answer to the vital question: 'Who is Jesus?' By their answer, however, inadequate, they separate themselves from other men, who think of Jesus in human terms (cf. v. 28 with 6.14 f.). Peter's 'confession' divides those who acknowledge Jesus as the Messiah from those who still do not recognize him. It seems doubtful whether Jesus was in fact concerned with his own 'messianic' status: for him, what was important was to proclaim God's coming kingdom. If the disciples did recognize him as God's anointed, we can understand the need for secrecy. His own role could easily be misunderstood, and divert men from his message. It was only when the Son of man had been raised from the dead (v. 31), that the question with which Mark constantly faces us came to the fore. The question which confronted men during Jesus' ministry—'What teaching is that?' became, after the cross and resurrection, the question 'Who then is this?' This is the question which still challenges us, as we read Mark's gospel.

Suggestions for further reading

C. F. D. Moule, *St. Mark* (Cambridge NEB Commentary).
D. E. Nineham, *St. Mark* (Penguin).
E. Schweizer, *The Good News according to Mark* (SPCK).
R. H. Fuller, *Interpreting the Miracles* (SCM).

Chapter 3

'The Son of man must suffer'
—St. Mark II

Mark *8.31–16.8.*

ST. MARK'S gospel has been aptly described as a passion narrative with a long introduction. We have already noted the way in which Mark, even in the early stages of his gospel, points his readers to the inevitable outcome of Jesus' ministry. The passion narrative proper begins in *14*.1, but the death of Jesus dominates the gospel from the point where he reaches Jerusalem in *11*.1; indeed, from as early as *8*.31, there are constant reminders of the suffering which lies ahead. If we compare Mark's gospel with those of Matthew and Luke, we see that though they give a similar amount of space to the death of Jesus, this makes up a smaller proportion of their books, because they give a great deal more space than Mark to the teaching of Jesus. The impact which each gospel makes upon its readers is therefore different. It is difficult for those of us who are familiar with the gospel material to appreciate just how the gospels would 'come across' to those who read them for the first time, but by reading through each of them in turn, we can perhaps grasp something of the very different flavour of these three books.

Read through Mk. *8.27–16*.8, once again trying to make your own outline of Mark's story, and noting how he is concerned throughout this section with the death of Jesus and with the meaning of discipleship.

Why has Mark chosen to emphasize the death of Jesus in this way? Various explanations have been given, not all of which are necessarily exclusive. It seems probable that there were certain pressures in the situation in which Mark found himself, and in the community for which he wrote, which caused him to write as he did. One obvious reason is the fact that for Jews, the idea of a crucified Messiah was a scandal and an offence (cf. 1 Cor. *1*.23); Christians had to show how a gospel which proclaimed Jesus as Messiah could make sense, and to do this they emphasized that the death of Jesus was part of God's plan—'necessary' and 'according to scripture' (see, e.g., the statement that the Son of man *must* suffer in Mk. *8*.31, and cf. *9*.12; *10*.38, 45; *14*.21). An alternative explanation suggests that Mark's emphasis on the Cross is due to the fact that Christians were already forgetting that their gospel was centred on a crucified Christ, and that Mark was therefore concerned to remind them of this fact: like Paul, he was determined to preach only 'Jesus Christ and him crucified' (1 Cor. *2*.2), and having demonstrated that Jesus is the Christ, he concentrated on the theme of the Cross.

It could be, however, that Mark's concern was primarily with the meaning of Christian discipleship rather than with Christology, and that this is why he links the sufferings of Jesus very closely with those of his followers. Here, too, commentators have offered alternative explanations: some have argued that Mark was writing at a time when Christians were suffering severe persecution, and that his aim was to remind them that disciples of a crucified Lord could expect no other fate. Others have suggested, on the contrary, that the Marcan community was a flourishing one, and needed to be reminded that Christian discipleship involved humility and suffering.

It will be seen how difficult it is to discover the precise situation in which a gospel was written, or to be confident that we understand why an evangelist felt he must stress certain themes. But it will be seen, also, that a gospel may be used and interpreted by Christians in circumstances very different from those of the community for whom it was first written, and still be found relevant.

The way of the Cross: teaching on discipleship

8.31–3. Jesus predicts his death. Ths section is closely linked with the preceding one, and for that reason is treated by many commentators as part of it. Yet it is undeniable that at this point the atmosphere of the gospel changes dramatically: from now on the dominant theme is that of the Cross. The sayings and stories which follow set out the way of Jesus as the way of the Cross; not only Jesus, but his disciples as well, must be prepared to give up everything, including life itself, for the sake of the kingdom.

It is difficult to believe that Jesus predicted his death and resurrection quite as clearly as Mark suggests. No doubt, as Christians of Mark's generation looked back on the ministry and death of Jesus, events fell into a pattern, and they felt more and more that everything must have been part of God's plan from the beginning. They assumed that Jesus must have shared this knowledge. Yet when we come to the passion story, we shall see that Jesus himself is not certain that his death is inevitable, and the disciples seem totally unprepared for what happens. Nevertheless, it seems incredible that Jesus should not have foreseen at least the likelihood of his death, or have gone to Jerusalem in full awareness of the probable outcome. It is likely that Jesus warned his disciples that both he and they must be prepared to face rejection, suffering and death, and at the same time expressed his confidence that God would ultimately vindicate them. But it is only natural that these sayings, as they are given us by Mark, reflect knowledge of later events, and so come across to us as precise predictions.

All the passion sayings refer to the sufferings, death and resurrection of the Son of man. In Dan. 7, the one like a Son of man symbolizes the saints of the Most High—i.e. those Jews who are faithful to God and to his Law—who are vindicated by God after a period of terrible suffering. The term is

49

therefore an appropriate one for Jesus to use when expressing his confident belief that God would vindicate him, even if men rejected and killed him: if Jesus is faithful to God, and to the mission which God has entrusted to him, God will be faithful to him.

Peter's reaction shows that the disciples are unable—or unwilling—to understand Jesus' teaching. Like the blind man at Bethsaida (8.22–26), their eyes have been only partly opened; it is not until after the resurrection that they see the whole truth.

8.34–9.1. *The way of discipleship.* There is obviously a close link with the previous section. Those who want to follow Jesus can do so only if they are prepared to accept his fate. The saying is a grim warning, for those who fail to acknowledge Jesus as their leader by following him and risking their lives with his, will in turn not be acknowledged as his disciples at the final judgement. Although v. 38 is put in negative terms, however, it implies also a promise that those who are prepared to follow Jesus through suffering and death will be vindicated by the Son of man when he enters into his glory, just as he himself is assured of vindication (v. 31); an alternative version of the saying in Matt. *10.*32 f. = Lk. *12.*8 f. in fact spells out this promise.

Jesus' words are presented as a challenge to the crowd (v. 34), as well as to those who are already his disciples. The self-denial which Jesus calls for is an attitude in which self-interest and personal desires are no longer central; the would-be disciple must be prepared to sacrifice everything if he is really to be a follower of Jesus.

The saying in 9.1 has a separate introduction ('And he said to them'), which suggests that it may once have been a separate saying. However, either Mark, or someone before him, has linked the saying about the coming of the Son of man in glory with this one about the coming of the kingdom of God. This verse is one of the most difficult in the gospel, partly because it seems to present us with an unfulfilled prophecy by Jesus. Centuries later, there is little sign that the kingdom of God has come with power. Many attempts have been made to solve this problem: the coming with power has been identified with the Transfiguration, the Resurrection, the coming of the Holy Spirit and the Fall of Jerusalem, but none of these events can be convincingly described as the coming of God's kingdom. C. H. Dodd attempted to solve the problem by suggesting that the saying should be translated as a promise that some of the bystanders would come to see that the kingdom of God had already come at some point before they became aware of it, but he failed to convince other scholars that the Greek verb used could express the idea of comprehension rather than physical sight. It is better to admit that the final coming of the kingdom in power which Jesus apparently expected has not taken place, although the vindication he confidently expected for himself and his followers has taken place, both at the Resurrection and in the course of history.

9.2–8. The Transfiguration. Mark links this story closely with what went before with the introductory phrase 'And after six days'; it is probable that he saw the glory of Jesus as a 'preview' of the glory which would be his when he had been vindicated, and that Mark believed that this was why the story could not be told until after Jesus' resurrection (v. 9). The temporal reference (unusual in Mark) may also be a reference to Ex. *24*.16, where Moses spends six days on the mountain before the Lord calls to him out of the cloud on the seventh. If such an allusion seems far-fetched, it must be remembered that it would have been of vital importance for the first Christians to demonstrate that Jesus was a greater figure than Moses, through whom God had revealed himself to the Jewish people. According to the story in Exodus, Moses spoke with God on the mountain, and when he came down the people were afraid to approach, because his face shone with reflected glory. Now Mark tells us that Jesus' whole appearance was transformed, and that when he came down from the mountain the crowds were amazed, though Mark does not explain why (v. 15). On Sinai, God spoke to Moses out of the cloud (Ex. *24*.16); now Mark tells us that the disciples saw a cloud, and that a voice came out of the cloud, saying 'Listen to

51

him', words which echo Moses' reference to a prophet like himself in Deut. *18*.15, 18.

It looks, then, as if Mark has told the story of the Transfiguration with one eye on the story of Moses. Moses himself appears in the narrative, together with Elijah. Various explanations of their presence have been offered: perhaps they are there as representatives of the Law and the Prophets; possibly they should be understood as forerunners of Jesus' suffering (cf. Mk. *9*.13 and Heb. *11*.26), encouraging Jesus as he contemplates his fate (cf. Lk. *9*.31); perhaps they are there because they, too, both experienced theophanies on mountains (cf. Ex. *24*; *33–4*; 1 Kings *19*). According to Mark, the three disciples also failed to understand the significance of Elijah and Moses. Once again it is Peter who demonstrates their lack of comprehension, for he wants to build three booths for Moses, Elijah and Jesus. No doubt he thinks he is honouring Jesus by ranking him with these two great figures of the past, but Peter, of all people, should have realized that Jesus is greater than 'Elijah or one of the prophets' (Mk. *8*.28). Moses and Elijah vanish from the scene, leaving only Jesus, and the disciples are commanded by the divine voice to listen to him. In the Old Testament, the command to listen is also the command to obey. The disciples are to obey Jesus because the authority given to him is greater than that given to any prophet; it is the authority of one who is uniquely Son of God (cf. Mk. *1*.11).

9.9–13. *Elijah and the Son of man.* Once again, we have a command for secrecy: the truth about Jesus, glimpsed by the disciples, will be made plain only by the paradoxical path of death and resurrection. Once again, the disciples fail to understand Jesus' words (v. 10); they cannot grasp what he says about resurrection, because they refuse to accept what he says about suffering and death. Their own question about Elijah suggests that they are thinking only of the final glory; there was a tradition that Elijah would come before the End (cf. Mal. *4*.5 f.). Jesus' reply links Elijah himself with suffering. Elijah has in fact already come—in the person of John the

Baptist; the fact that he has been rejected and killed is a sure indication that the same fate will befall the Son of man.

9.14–29. A dumb spirit is driven out. The emphasis in this story is on the need for faith. The vital question now is not so much concerned with the authority of Jesus to heal—though that is clearly demonstrated—as with the believing response of men. As Mark tells the story, it demonstrates in fact men's failure to respond: the scribes are found arguing with the disciples, the disciples are unable to heal the child, and the father's faith in Jesus' ability to help him is far from secure (v. 23). This general failure calls forth Jesus' despairing cry in v. 19. The climax of the story comes in v. 24: in Mark's eyes, the father's appeal is typical of those who do respond to Jesus, for like the disciples who half see the truth, this man half believes in Jesus.

The child is described as being possessed by a spirit, and this was the natural explanation of his symptoms in first-century Palestine; on the evidence given here, we would be more likely to diagnose epilepsy. But it is as misleading to try to explain Mark's story in twentieth-century terms as it is to try to cling to first-century views when coping with the world today. If we want to understand the significance of the miracle for Mark, we shall have to try to enter into his world and see things in his terms; but if we want to understand the relevance of faith in Christ for our modern world, we need to use the thought-forms of today, not those of the first century.

9.30–2. Jesus again predicts his death. This second prediction of the passion is the least detailed, and possibly the most authentic. The verb translated 'delivered' is ambiguous: it can mean either 'betrayed' (as in *3.19*) or 'handed over' (as in Rom. *8.32*). In the absence of any other details about the passion of Jesus, the word probably refers here, not to the betrayal by Judas, but to the purpose of God: harsh as it may seem to us, Mark seems to be saying that the Son of man will be delivered up by God into the hands of men. Once again, the disciples are unable to understand Jesus' words, and are afraid—a typical reaction in Mark.

53

9.33–7. *True greatness.* The disciples now demonstrate their failure to understand Jesus' words by arguing among themselves about their own status. The reply of Jesus in v. 35 is typical: true greatness is demonstrated in humility. The 'acted parable' of the child in vv. 36–7 does not fit this theme, and it is interesting to notice that it would fit the context much better if it were found at *10*.15—just as the saying at *10*.15 would fit much better here! Matthew seems to agree, since in his discussion about greatness in *18*.1–4 he uses a saying parallel to Mk. *10*.15. It looks very much as though the two sayings about children may have been mixed up at the oral stage of the tradition.

9.38–40. *For and against Jesus.* This story is of interest to Mark because it is on the theme of discipleship, and underlines the all-important distinction between being for Jesus or . against him.

9.41–50. *Sayings about life and death.* This collection of sayings on the theme of reward and punishment is addressed to the disciples. Like the teaching in *8*.34–8, the emphasis is on the vital importance of the decision with which Jesus confronts men; it is worth giving up everything else for the sake of the kingdom of God.

The word 'Christ' is used in v. 41 as a name. This is strange since elsewhere in Mark, 'Christ' is used as a title, but not as a name. The explanation is that on this one occasion the term has been read back into the tradition. It is interesting to notice how rarely this has happened. Although the phrase obviously reflects the standpoint of the Christian community, the saying itself has an authentic ring (cf. Matt. *25*.31–46).

Verses 44 and 46 are absent from many manuscripts, and are probably late additions to the text.

10.1–12. *A question about divorce.* Jesus once again addresses the crowds but the significance of his teaching is spelt out for the disciples afterwards. The incident is relevant to a section on the meaning of discipleship, because Jesus contrasts the concessions for divorce allowed by the Law with its basic, rigorous demand: those who follow Jesus are those whose aim is to do the will of God, not to look for loopholes in the Law. There seems to have been considerable debate among Jesus' contemporaries as to the grounds on which a man was entitled to divorce his wife: the disciples of Rabbi Hillel permitted a man to divorce his wife on trivial grounds, whereas the more conservative disciples of Rabbi Shammai insisted that adultery alone was a sufficient cause. The question dealt with here is much more radical, however—namely, is divorce permitted at all? The question is put to Jesus by Pharisees 'in order to test him', which probably means they were trying to trap him into speaking against the Law. Jesus, however, does not dispute the validity of the rule set out in Deut. *24*.1; he sees it as a concession which does not affect the basic principle set out in Gn. *1*.27 and *2*.7. There is no suggestion here that God commanded one thing and Moses another, since all three passages would have been understood as teaching given through Moses; the concession in Deuteronomy was given because of the hardness of men's hearts, but the disciples should not expect such concessions.

The suggestion that a husband could commit adultery against his wife (v. 11) must have been as startling as the idea that a wife might divorce her husband (v. 12), since in Jewish Law adultery was committed only against the husband, and a woman could not divorce her husband. In the first saying, Jesus extends to women the status which Judaism had confined to men; the second saying has perhaps been adapted to conditions in a society where Roman law gave women the right to divorce their husbands, since there would have been no point in Jesus denouncing something which could not take place under Jewish Law.

10.13–16. *Jesus blesses the children.* This story has been used from earliest times to support the practice of infant baptism, but for Mark its importance probably lay in the sayings about the kingdom of God in vv. 14 and 15, since these sum up the humble attitude required of disciples. The disciples themselves, however, once again demonstrate their failure to understand Jesus' teaching by trying to keep the children away: but it is the children, unconcerned with their own status and privileges, to whom the kingdom belongs.

10.17–31. *A rich man loses eternal life, but others find it.* This section consists of what may once have been four separate items; by placing them together, Mark confronts us once again with the demands of discipleship.

In vv. 17–22 we have the story of the rich man who found the demands too great. Mark tells us only that he was rich, Matthew describes him as young, and Luke tells us that he was a ruler—hence the usual description of him as the rich young ruler. Both his gesture in kneeling to Jesus, and his form of address (Good Teacher), seem extravagant, but Jesus' reaction in v. 21 suggests that the man was sincere. He wants to know how he can inherit eternal life—another way of talking about entering the kingdom of God; notice how the two phrases alternate in this section (cf. vv. 23–5, 30). Jesus' question in v. 18 has caused many problems; already Matthew found it difficult, and altered the wording (cf. Matt. *19*.17). Because of its difficulty, the saying has a considerable claim to authenticity; moreover, it is typical of Jesus to point men away from himself to the character and demands of God. Yet it is also typical of Mark that these demands should confront us in the person of Jesus himself; the crucial test of a man's obedience is whether or not he is prepared to give up everything and follow Jesus. Although this man recognized that obedience to the commandments was not enough, his approach to religion is similar to that of the Pharisees in vv. 1–9, concerned to ask 'How much need I do?' He lacks the single-hearted love of God which is prepared to fling everything away.

The sayings about wealth in vv. 23–7 spell out the significance of this incident for the benefit of the disciples. The rich find it difficult to enter the kingdom of God because they are not prepared to exchange all they have for the one thing that matters. The saying in v. 25 may well be proverbial; commentators have shown great ingenuity in trying to make it mean something else, but it seems likely that Jesus wished to make

his hearers think by presenting them with an absurd picture of
the largest animal they knew trying to go through the tiniest
possible hole. The disciples, however, are simply astonished;
once again, they show themselves totally unable to understand Jesus' teaching.

Verses 28–30 make an appropriate contrast to the story in
vv. 17–22; Peter and his companions have responded to the
call which the rich man rejects. We are reminded here both of
the cost of discipleship and its rewards.

The section closes with a saying which does not fit very well
at this point, and which is found in other contexts in Matthew
and Luke (Matt. *20*.16; Luke *13*.30).

10.32–4. Jesus predicts his death for the third time. This prediction is much fuller than the earlier two, and contains precise details which seem to reflect a knowledge of the passion
story. Jesus is now on the road which will take him to
Jerusalem, and once again his followers are amazed and
afraid. In one sense this can be described as the beginning of
the passion narrative, and it is noticeable that in the incidents
that follow, Jesus makes no attempt to conceal his 'messianic
claims'; the true identity of Jesus becomes clearer for Mark
the closer we move to the Cross.

10.35–45. The cost of discipleship. Like the previous passion
predictions, this one is followed by an incident which shows
the failure of the disciples to grasp his teaching. The request
of James and John that Jesus should do for them whatever
they ask shows how far they are from understanding him; they
think they have a right to demand a reward. What they have in
mind is nothing less than the best positions in the messianic
kingdom which they believe Jesus is about to set up; they
think of the future in terms of glory, and forget the suffering
which must come first.

Jesus' reply once again reminds them of the necessity for
suffering. Readers of Mark's gospel know that the cup which
Jesus drinks is the cup of suffering (cf. *14*.36); the reference
to baptism reminds us of the waters which overwhelm one—
a familiar Old Testament image for calamities. The two
disciples declare that they are ready to share Jesus' cup and

baptism, but clearly do not understand what they are promising, any more than they understood what they were asking (v. 38). The request to sit at the right and left of Jesus reminds us inevitably of the account of the death of Jesus between two robbers; it is through suffering that Jesus comes into his glory.

The saying in v. 42 links the request of James and John with the theme of authority, and v. 43 is reminiscent of teaching found in *8*.35, *9*.35 and *10*.31. In v. 45, however, we have a new idea, since for the first time we have a saying about the significance of Jesus' death; up to this point, we have learned only that it is necessary. This verse has been the subject of more discussion than any other in Mark's gospel. Does it go back to Jesus himself, or does it reflect the beliefs of the early Christian community? What is the background of the interpretation of the death of Jesus as a ransom? Most commentators have assumed that the saying reflects Isaiah *53*, and have spoken of Jesus' self-identification with the Suffering Servant. In fact, the vocabulary and ideas used here are quite different from those found in Isa. *53*: instead of the Servant of God who dies as a guilt-offering we have the Son of man who gives his life as a ransom. The true background of the statement that the Son of man came not to be served but to serve is probably to be found in the idea of the Son of man itself. The saying is as paradoxical as the one which precedes it in v. 44, for the Son of man in Dan. *7* is the one who is given authority to rule over others: as usual, Jesus comes out with the opposite of what men expect. At the same time, however, he is pointing to what is implicit in Dan. *7*, for before the righteous (represented by the Son of man) are given authority to rule, they are subjected to suffering and oppression. Moreover, the idea that the suffering and death of the martyrs could play a role in the redemption of Israel is not unknown in Judaism at this time (cf. 4 Macc. *6*.27; *17*.22). Although Mk. *10*.45 has no parallel in the rest of the gospel, it is the logical conclusion of many of Jesus' earlier paradoxical statements.

10.46–52. *A blind man sees the way.* This is the last healing miracle in the gospel, and like the healing of the blind man in ch. *8*, it has a double meaning. Bartimaeus may be blind, but he sees enough of the truth to address Jesus as 'Son of David'. this time it is the crowd, not Jesus, which tries to silence him; the time has come for Jesus' identity to be made known, but the crowd are blind. Jesus commends the man's faith, which has healed him; and Bartimaeus follows him on the way—to Jerusalem—the way of discipleship.

The King comes to Jerusalem

11.1–11. *Jesus rides into Jerusalem.* Mark has told us nothing of previous visits by Jesus to Jerusalem, but it is possible that he had been there before, and possibly taught there. Apart from the evidence of the Fourth gospel, there are hints in the synoptics of an earlier visit (e.g. Lk. *13*.34). One possibility is that Mark has telescoped two visits; certainly the period between Jesus' arrival in Jerusalem and the crucifixion may have been longer that the five days assigned to it in the Church's calendar.

The crowd may have been made up of pilgrims arriving in the city for the Passover. Although Mark understands Jesus' arrival as the coming of the king to Jerusalem, the incident does not seem to have been an unambiguous messianic demonstration. No reference is made to it in the charges brought against Jesus at the trial, and John tells us that the disciples did not understand its significance until later (Jn. *12*.16). Jesus is said to have ridden on a young donkey in fulfilment of Zech. *9*.9, but it is unlikely that this would have been interpreted as a messianic claim at the time. Even the cries of the crowd are the normal shouts of praise and greeting at a festival. For Mark, then, Jesus enters the city as king, heralded by a blind beggar by the roadside, and welcomed by the unconscious plaudits of the crowd.

The fact that the animal had never been ridden made it suitable for a sacred purpose. It is not clear how we should understand the reference to 'the Lord' in v. 3. In the Old Testament the phrase is used of God, but that meaning does not suit the context here. Possibly it means 'the owner', which would be a logical reply, especially if the animal's owner was understood to be with Jesus. Alternatively, the phrase may be used in the sense which it came to have in the Christian community, meaning Jesus himself; if so, the title has been read back into the ministry of Jesus here and nowhere else in Mark. The words of the crowd come from Ps. *118*.25, where they are a welcome to those who come to the feast: for Mark however, Jesus is the one who comes in the name of the Lord in a unique sense.

In Jerusalem, Jesus inspects the temple, but in contrast to the story in Luke (*19*.45), does nothing at this stage.

11.12–26. *Israel's failure.* The action of Jesus in the temple is placed by Mark on the following day, and he brings out its significance by sandwiching the incident within another story—a device which he uses elsewhere in order to illuminate one story by means of another. We are clearly meant to see a link between the fate of the barren fig tree and Jesus' condemnation of what was taking place in the temple.

The incident of the fig tree is a difficult one. It is the only 'negative' miracle in the gospels, and as such seems out of character for Jesus. Whatever the origins of the story, it is used symbolically by Mark: the fig tree represents Israel, which has failed to produce the appropriate fruit (cf. Jer. *8*.13). Inevitably, judgement will follow. It overtakes the fig tree before the evening.

Mark places the so-called cleansing of the temple at the end of the ministry, John at the beginning. We cannot tell which dating is correct in terms of chronology. Mark records no other visit of Jesus to Jerusalem, so there is no other setting which he can give it. Both Mark and John place the incident at a Passover. More important than the dating is the theological setting which the evangelists give the incident. John sets the theme for his gospel with this story—a symbol of the way in which Jesus had replaced the temple as the focus of worship. Mark places the incident at the end of Jesus' life, as the climax of his challenge to the Jewish religious authorities and the Jewish nation; the incident is a judgement on Judaism, and a sign of the destruction which will overtake Jerusalem, but it also sets the seal on Jesus' own fate (v. 18). Jesus' action has sometimes been understood as an attack on the sacrificial system, but the quotation from Isa. 56.7 and Jer. 7.11 in v. 17 suggests that it is the misuse of the sacrificial system which Jesus was attacking. The outward niceties of religion, meant to ensure that animals were without blemish and temple taxes were paid in the right currency, led to the realities being ignored; Jesus condemns the priests for an attitude similar to that of the scribes, and it is not surprising if priests and scribes plot together against him.

The end of the story of the fig tree is briefly told. If it is a pointer to the judgement which is coming on Israel, we can understand why the disciples are told, in the face of coming disaster, to have faith in God. The sayings in vv. 23–6 are probably later additions to the story.

11.27–33. The authority of Jesus. This is the first of a group of conflict stories. In this one, representatives of all the religious authorities in Jerusalem challenge him on the question of his own authority. Jesus turns the attack by asking them about the authority of John the Baptist. There is a real link between the two questions, for we have seen the way in which Mark presents John the Baptist as the forerunner of Jesus: the source of their authority must therefore be the same. Because the religious leaders refused to believe John, they of course refuse to believe Jesus also. They cannot answer Jesus' question, and he will not answer theirs, but the answer has of course been spelt out for us already throughout Mark's gospel.

12.1–12. The parable of the vineyard. Jesus once again uses a parable, but this time, instead of mystifying his hearers, its meaning is said to be all too clear to them (v. 12). No doubt they would have been familiar with Isaiah's image of Israel as God's vineyard (Isa. 5.1–7). New Testament scholars have been inclined to insist that none of Jesus' parables were intended to be understood as allegories—i.e., we are not meant to give a specific meaning to all the characters and details in a story. There is no reason, however, why Jesus should *not* have used allegory on occasion, and there is plenty of symbolism in the Old Testament, even more in apocalyptic writings, where animals, e.g., are used to represent people. In this story, Mark has clearly interpreted the tenants of the vineyard as representing the leaders of Israel, and the servants as the prophets sent to them by God; now they are confronted, in Jesus, with their final opportunity, and if they reject him, then the inheritance will be taken from them and given to others. There is no reason to suppose that Mark has misunderstood the meaning of Jesus' story, though no doubt by the time he wrote, some details had taken on new significance, and others had been added: the last messenger, e.g., is the owner's son—and by Mark's time, Jesus was acknowledged in the Christian community as God's Son; the owner of the vineyard is said to come and destroy the tenants—an unlikely detail in the original story, but understandable if it was added in the light of later events. Matthew and Luke have added further details; the simplest version of the story is found in the Gospel of Thomas (*65*).

The quotation from Ps. *118* is not particularly appropriate to the parable itself, but was a favourite proof-text in the early Church (cf. Acts *4*.11; 1 Pet. *2*.7), and presumably it has been added here to 'reverse' the rejection of the son in v. 8.

12.13–17. *A question about taxes*. The question is a deliberate trap; the tax referred to was imposed on all the inhabitants of the country, and was resented as a sign of their subjection to Rome. If Jesus replies that the tax should be paid, he will lose popular support; if he replies that it should not, he can be charged with sedition. Jesus' answer is not just a clever escape from the trap. He treats the question as unimportant, compared with the far more vital question of men's response to the demands of God.

12.18–27. *A question about the resurrection*. The Sadducees (the priestly party) did not believe in a future resurrection, since they argued that it was not scriptural—i.e., it was not found in the five books of Moses, the only books whose authority they recognized. Belief in a future life seems to have developed comparatively late in Jewish thought, but it was held by the Pharisees, among others. The Sadducees' question here is meant to demonstrate that the provisions of the Law in Deut. 25.5 ff. for levirate marriage exclude the doctrine of resurrection.

Jesus first of all rejects their crude understanding of resurrection (v. 25), and then demonstrates that the Law itself implies the doctrine of resurrection (vv. 26 f.).

12.28–34. A question about the commandments. For once, the questioner is not hostile to Jesus. Similar questions seem to have been debated regularly by the rabbis. Jesus' answer is taken from scripture. Instead of one commandment, he offers two, for it is only as men love their neighbour that they know what it is to love God, and it is only if they love God that they are able to love their neighbour.

12.35–7. Jesus asks a question. The question raised here was probably one which was debated between the first Christians and their fellow Jews. The quotation is from Ps. *110*, which was believed to have been composed by David: how was it, then, that David could address the Messiah here as 'Lord', if the Messiah was in fact his own descendant, since a son is always subject to his father? In its present form, this question seems to reflect tension between two Christian beliefs—that Jesus was 'Son of David', and that he was greater than David. The passage should not be understood as denying the Davidic descent of Jesus. The point is that the Lordship of Jesus is much more important than his descent from David.

12.38–40. Warning against the scribes. It would be wrong to assume that all scribes were guilty of hypocrisy. Although there were some who made a parade of their piety, others were sincerely concerned to do God's will (cf. vv. 28–34).

12.41–44. A widow's gift. This story forms a contrast to the previous section, by providing an example of true piety.

13. Future suffering and vindication. This long discourse follows on Jesus' prediction in v. 2 that the temple will be completely destroyed. Four of the disciples ask Jesus when this will happen, and how they may know when the End is near (vv. 3–4). Jesus warns them to expect various disasters, but tells them that these calamities are *not* signs of the End (vv. 5–8). He then warns them of the suffering which will come to them because they are his disciples—they, too, can expect to be tried and delivered up to death (vv. 9–13). All this must happen before the End draws near.

It is only when 'the desolating sacrilege' is set up that the inhabitants of Judea must flee to the hills (v. 14). Mark himself clearly realized that his warning is cryptic, since he adds the comment 'Let the reader understand'. The phrase is in fact taken from Daniel (e.g. *11*.31), where it referred to a pagan altar set up by Antiochus Epiphanes in the temple, and presumably it refers to a similar kind of desecration here. When the temple is desecrated, this will be the sign that the traumas of the End have arrived (vv. 14–23). The disaster will be of such magnitude that sun, moon and stars will be overcome by darkness (vv. 24 f.). But this will be the moment when the Son of man gathers together the elect: those who endure suffering are finally vindicated (vv. 26 f.).

The parable of the fig-tree shows that there will be signs by which Jesus' followers can know when these things are about to happen (vv. 28–31). Nevertheless, the exact time is not known—even to Jesus himself (v. 32). There is therefore need to keep up constant vigilance, a point illustrated by the parable of the absent landlord (vv. 33–7).

It is easy to see how relevant this teaching would have been to the situation of many first-century Christians. Many of them expected Jesus to return in glory very soon—and here they would find the warning 'Not yet!' (vv. 4 f.). Many of them had to face persecution and death for their faith—and here they would find encouragement (vv. 9–13) and the promise of final victory (vv. 26 f.). Sometimes they would wonder whether their troubles would ever end, and the answer given here is 'Yes' (vv. 28–31); sometimes they would try to calculate the date, and the advice given here is 'Don't' (v. 32); sometimes they would decide that nothing would ever happen—and the warning given here is 'Watch' (vv. 33–7).

Death and resurrection

14.1–11. The anointing of Jesus. Mark does not tell us what motives led the woman to do what she did, but he supplies an explanation in the comment by Jesus: unknowingly, she has anointed his body for burial. Since she is said to have poured the perfume on Jesus' head, Mark probably intends us to interpret her action also as the anointing of Jesus as king: it is through his death that Jesus is to be proclaimed as the anointed one, the Messiah.

The story is set in the context of the plot against Jesus by the religious authorities and by Judas (vv. 1 f., 10 f.).

14.12–16. Preparation for the passover. Mark clearly understands the Last Supper to have been a passover meal (v. 12), though he says nothing about the preparation of the passover lamb. John gives a different dating, placing the festival one day later; according to him, Jesus died on passover day itself (Jn. *18*.28), at the very moment when the passover lambs were killed. It is impossible now to decide which dating is correct. Each evangelist, in his own way, makes use of the passover theme to say something about the significance of Jesus' death—Mark, by interpreting the Last Supper as a passover meal, and John by presenting Jesus himself as the true passover lamb (cf. 1 Cor. *5*.7).

14.17–25. The Last Supper. The saying about Judas emphasizes, at one and the same time, that the death of Jesus can be understood as part of God's purpose, but that this does not exonerate those who were humanly responsible for his death from blame.

Verses 22–5 should be compared with 1 Cor. *11*.23–5, as well as with Matt. *26*.26–9 and Lk. *22*.15–20. The accounts vary in their details, and we cannot be certain which is the earliest form of words. The central themes of the story as it now stands are, however, clear. Jesus breaks the bread and invites the disciples to share it. The cup of wine is interpreted as a symbol of the blood of the covenant between God and his people, a covenant which points forward to a time of fulfilment in the kingdom of God. It was probably the Pauline tradition which added the word 'new' to 'covenant', but the idea is implied in Mark. God's covenant with his people (no longer Israel alone) is now sealed by the death of Jesus, not the death of animals.

14.26–31. Prophecy of the denial. Jesus' prophecy of the disciples' failure contains a promise that they will nevertheless continue to be his followers (v. 28).

14.32–42. Gethsemane. The three disciples who shared the vision on the mountain (9.2–8) should have been most able to share Jesus' agony, but once again they fail him. Like the tradition in Heb. 5.7, this story stresses the real anguish of Jesus as he approached death. The word 'Abba', meaning 'Father', is an intimate form of address, and no parallel to it has been found in Jewish prayers. In Rom. 8.15 and Gal. 4.6, Paul says that Christians have received the spirit of the Son, enabling them to call God 'Abba'; this suggests that the term was remembered as typical of Jesus.

14.43–52. The arrest. These verses underline the hideous nature of Judas' action in betraying his friend with a kiss.

14.53–65. The trial before the sanhedrin. Mark's account of Jesus' examination by the Jewish authorities emphasizes his innocence; they could find no evidence against him—even their attempts to bring false evidence collapsed! Jesus himself is silent, until challenged to say whether or not he is the anointed one and Son of the Blessed—an unusual title, not found elsewhere. Ironically, the high priest's unbelieving question reveals the truth about Jesus' identity. Now at last Jesus openly acknowledges that he is the Messiah, but immediately speaks of his future acknowledgement as the Son of man (cf. Dan. 7.13 and Ps. *110*.1). At the very moment when he is condemned to die, he declares his own confidence that God will vindicate him.

14.54, 66–72. *Peter's denial.* This story forms a 'sandwich' round that of Jesus' trial, contrasting Peter's failure with Jesus' steadfastness. In spite of the warning in *8*.38, Peter is ashamed of Jesus.

15.1–15. *The trial before Pilate.* Pilate behaves here in a way which is uncharacteristic of what we read of him elsewhere; Mark portrays him as indecisive, anxious to please the Jews, afraid to administer justice. Mark is concerned to show that it was the Jews, rather than the Romans, who were responsible for Jesus' death, even though he died at the hands of Roman soldiers. According to him, Pilate was pushed into a position where he was forced to act, because the Sanhedrin had brought a political charge against Jesus. Nothing is known of the custom described in v. 6.

15.16–20. *Mockery.* The irony of this story is that the mocking soldiers 'honour' Jesus for what he really is. It is through suffering that he is proclaimed as king.

15.21–39. *The crucifixion.* Once again, the truth is proclaimed through Jesus' passion—this time, in what is written up in derision (v. 26). The early church was quick to see his death as 'in accordance with the scriptures', and the story of the crucifixion contains echoes of Ps. *22* in vv. 24, 31 and 34. Christians have often found it difficult to think of Jesus dying with a cry of despair on his lips, but Mark is not afraid to present this picture of Jesus sharing the depths of human suffering, knowing not only physical pain but the agony of feeling forsaken by God himself. These words are a profound expression of the significance of Jesus' suffering, for if he experienced the depths of human doubt and desolation, then others who know doubt and despair may share the faith with which he nevertheless appealed to the God who seemed to have deserted him.

At the moment of Jesus' death, Mark tells us, the curtain in the temple which hung before the Holy of Holies was torn in two (v. 38). He is, of course, thinking symbolically, but we cannot be certain whether he means that the death of Jesus opens up the way for men to approach God (cf. Heb. *10.*19f.), or whether he sees it as sealing the fate of Judaism (cf. v.29).

And as Jesus dies, he is acknowledged as 'son of God', not by a Jew but by a Gentile, who is one of his executioners.

*15.*40–7. *The burial.* The story of the burial serves to confirm the death of Jesus (vv. 44 f.). Since the disciples have all fled, it is left to a sympathetic member of the sanhedrin to bury Jesus, and women are the only followers of Jesus to witness his death (vv. 40 f.) and his burial (v. 47).

*16.*1–8. *Resurrection.* The story of the women at the tomb forms an abrupt ending to the gospel. Many have supposed that Mark intended to write more, or that the ending has been lost—including the unknown authors who made two attempts to round the gospel off (see the 'longer' ending, vv. 9–20, and the 'shorter' in the mg.). It may be, however, that it is because we have read the other gospels, which all end with accounts of appearances of the risen Lord, that we assume that Mark is incomplete. It is entirely typical of his gospel that when the women are confronted with the news of the greatest of God's acts—the resurrection of Jesus from the dead—they are overcome by trembling and astonishment. Perhaps Mark thinks that his readers should not need to ask for anything more than this: after all, he is writing for those who know the risen Christ, and he has taken the story up to the point where their own experience begins.

The conversation among the women about the stone seems a little naive, but it serves to underline the emptiness of the tomb. The message of the young man is sent to the disciples and Peter (v. 7) because Peter has denied that he is a disciple. Nevertheless, though they have all failed him, Jesus summons them to follow him back to Galilee, where he first called them. His resurrection means restoration for them also.

Read *Groundwork* 31a–c.

Suggestion for further reading

R. H. Lightfoot, *The Gospel Message of St. Mark* (OUP).

Chapter 4

The True Israel—St. Matthew

Passages for special study:

Matthew *4*.1–17; *5–7*; *8*.1–17; *12*.38–42; *16*.13–22; *21*.28–22.14; *23*; *24*.45–25.46; *27*.57–28.20.

ANYONE who reads through Matthew's gospel for the first time, after previously reading through Mark, would experience the sensation of retracing familiar ground. Although Matthew includes many stories which are not found in Mark, a great deal of his material is very similar to that used by Mark, so much so that at times the wording is identical. It is clear that there is some literary relationship between the two documents; either Mark has used Matthew, or Matthew has used Mark, or both of them have used a third document. The earliest suggestion (made by Augustine) was that Mark abbreviated Matthew, and there are still some scholars who argue that Matthew is our first gospel, and was used as a basis of their own gospels by both Mark and Luke. However, the most commonly held theory today is that Mark is the earliest of the gospels, and was used as a basis by both Matthew and Luke. Because these three gospels are so similar they are known as the Synoptic gospels (from a Greek word meaning 'seeing together') and the study of the relationship between them is known as 'source criticism'. (See *Groundwork* 15 f.)

At one time, scholars assumed that the main reason why Matthew's gospel is so much longer than Mark's was that Matthew had access to a great deal of material which was not available to Mark. While it is probably true that each evangelist had his own source or sources, we cannot assume that Mark did not know any of the traditions which he did not include but which are used in the other gospels. The evangelists did not work like stamp-collectors, including everything of value which came their way, and leaving on one side only obvious duplicates; rather they chose to use material which fitted into their particular plan and which illustrated the point which they were trying to emphasize. As we have seen already in the case of Mark, the gospels are not simply collections of stories about Jesus, but are theological documents in their own right. If Matthew has chosen—as he has done—to include a great deal more of the teaching of Jesus than has Mark, then it is important to ask why he has done so, and not simply where he found it.

Questions about the way in which the evangelists handled the tradition—what they decided to include, whether they adapted it, the order in which they arranged it, how they linked the various stories together, what they decided to emphasize—are known as 'redaction criticism'. (See *Groundwork* 15r). Clearly in thinking about an author's purpose, it is necessary to look at his book as a whole, and not at parts of it. Although the notes given here are on selected portions only, students should read through the whole of Matthew's gospel with the following outline as a guide.

1–2	*Introduction* (See notes above, pp. 15–17)
	1.1–17 Genealogy
	18–25 Birth of Jesus
	2.1–12 Visit of the magi
	13–23 Flight to Egypt and return
3	*Ministry of John the Baptist*
	3.1–12 Message of John
	13–17 Baptism of Jesus
4	*Jesus begins his ministry*
	4.1–11 Testing of God's Son
	12–17 Jesus begins to preach
	18–22 Jesus calls his first disciples
	23–5 Summary of Jesus' activity
5–7	*Sermon on the Mount*

Notes on passages for special study

4.1–11. Jesus is tested by the devil. Matthew fills out the brief summary given by Mark; whereas Mark is content merely to note that Jesus has done battle with Satan, Matthew is concerned with the nature of the temptation. Notice how the first two temptations begin from the premise 'If you are the Son of God', taking up the words of the heavenly voice in *3*.17; in both cases, the temptation is to demand that God use his power to show special favour to his Son; in the second case, it is backed up by a promise from the psalms that God will protect his people. Those who succumb to the temptation to use God for their own purposes are in fact not honouring God at all, but furthering their own interests: hence the apparently strange third temptation to worship the devil.

The three replies given by Jesus all come in the form of a quotation from scripture, and it is significant that they are all taken from the story of Israel's journey in the wilderness—in other words, the time when Israel was tested by God himself, and failed the test (Deut. 8.3; 6.16, 13). Again and again God's people fell into the trap of expecting favourable treatment from God. It looks very much, therefore, as though the significance of the story for Matthew is that in contrast to Israel, who failed repeatedly to obey God, Jesus has withstood temptation. Jesus proves himself a true Son of God, obedient to God's will.

This story is often treated as the account of Jesus' inner struggle to discover the meaning of his messiahship; whether or not that was how it originated it is now impossible to say. As it is now written, it has been shaped to give us theological information about Jesus, not autobiographical details of his vocation.

4.12–17. *Jesus returns to Galilee.* It is typical of Matthew that he sees Jesus' arrival in Galilee to begin his ministry as the fulfilment of Old Testament prophecy. The population of Galilee was mixed, part Jewish and part Gentile; hence the scathing description 'Galilee of the Gentiles'. As far as we know, Jesus confined his ministry in Galilee to Jews; Matthew himself tells us that Jesus taught in synagogues (4.23), instructed his disciples not to preach and heal among the Gentiles or Samaritans (10.5–6) and agreed to heal Gentiles only because of the exceptional faith of those who interceded for them (8.5–13; 15.21–8). Nevertheless, Matthew interprets Jesus' mission in Galilee, to those on the borders of Judaism, as a fulfilment of God's promise to bring light to those in darkness, and as a pointer towards the future salvation of the Gentiles.

The Sermon on the Mount (5–7)

For Matthew, the teaching of Jesus is of central importance: notice how for him the first great event of Jesus' ministry is the Sermon on the Mount. Matthew gathers a great deal of the teaching of Jesus into five blocks: *5–7, 10, 13, 18, 23–5*, each of which ends with the words 'When Jesus had finished. . . .' Some scholars have argued that Matthew was trying to make a deliberate parallel between the words of Jesus and the five books of Moses, but there is no correspondence with the subject matter of Genesis—Deuteronomy.

In *5–7*, however, it is clear that Matthew does intend a contrast with Moses. In describing how Jesus taught on the mountain, he no doubt remembered that according to Ex. *19*.20 ff. the Law was given to Moses on Mount Sinai. But whereas Moses received the Law on the mountain, and then came down to the people to hand it over to them, Jesus himself gives the 'new law' to the disciples from the mountain. Although Moses was venerated as the great Lawgiver, he was in fact only an intermediary, receiving and passing on the Law; in Jesus, a greater than Moses is here!

A comparison with Luke's Sermon on the Plain (Lk. *6*.17–49) shows many similarities between the two discourses, but Matthew has included far more material than Luke. The fact that Matthew places Jesus on a hill, while Luke puts him at its foot, is not of any geographical interest. We have seen that Matthew's 'mountain' is of theological significance, and it is possible that Luke also has the parallel with Moses in mind, since according to his account Jesus went into the hills to pray, and then returned to the foot of the hill to teach there.

5.1 f. *Introduction.* Jesus sits to teach; this is characteristic of a Jewish rabbi. What he says is addressed to those who are disciples—though the crowd, in the background, apparently overhears (cf. *7*.28 f.): they, too, may be disciples if they wish.

5.3–10. *The Beatitudes.* Jesus is here making statements of fact, rather than pronouncing blessings; these are the people who are *really* blessed, or happy. Note that in Luke's version (*6*.20 ff.), it is the disciples who are said to be blessed ('you poor', etc.), and the Beatitudes are balanced by Woes. Whereas Luke interprets poverty and hunger literally,

Matthew understands them spiritually. The qualities of those whom Jesus declares to be blessed are illustrated in his own life; and they ought to be characteristic of his disciples, too.

'Those who know that they are poor' expresses the meaning of the words traditionally translated 'poor in spirit'; the phrase refers to those who recognize their poverty over against the riches of God—not to those who are in any way lacking in spirit. In the Old Testament, 'the poor' is often used to mean 'the righteous'.

'The Kingdom of Heaven' in Matthew has the same meaning as 'The Kingdom of God' elsewhere. It was characteristic of Judaism to avoid using the name of God, and the evangelist continually demonstrates his Jewish background in his choice of language and his use of the Old Testament.

Those who are sorrowful, because of the present disobedience of the world, 'shall find consolation' when the kingdom comes (cf. Isa. *61*.2). The Greek verb is passive (cf. the familiar 'they shall be comforted')—a way of referring to the activity of God.

'Those of a gentle spirit' are those who do not try to seize authority and power for themselves, and whose concern is for others. The traditional English translation, 'meek', has unfortunate associations which are by no means referred to in this verse. In Hebrew thought, proud men have seized the earth for their possession, but in the end, God will give it to the gentle in spirit, who submit to his rule (cf. Ps. *37*.11).

'Those who hunger and thirst to see right prevail' long for the time when the way of God will be vindicated—i.e. when God's Kingdom will be established, and all men acknowledge his rule. The language about hungering and thirsting and being satisfied echoes the Old Testament picture of the final age as a great banquet.

The principle that those who show mercy will receive mercy is repeated in *6*.14, and illustrated in *18*.23–35.

For us, the heart symbolizes emotion, but for the Jew, it was the centre of thought and will. 'Those whose hearts are pure' are therefore those whose lives are governed by the desire to do the will of God. To 'see God' means to come into his presence; only those whose lives reflect the character of God can truly worship him (cf. Ps. *24*.3–4; *51*.10 f.).

Those who make peace will be called the sons of God. To be a son of someone means to be like him, and to make peace is to be like God. Although God's intention for mankind is that they should be his children, made 'in his image' and reflecting his character, this purpose has been obscured by man's rebellion; but the announcement of the Kingdom means God's willingness to adopt men and women as his children.

Those who are obedient to the will of God may well be persecuted as a result—but the Kingdom is theirs. This promise rounds off the section, by echoing the words of the opening saying in verse 5.

5.11–12. *Persecution*. These verses are a similar saying on the theme of persecution, this time addressed directly to the disciples; they may suffer 'for my sake'— i.e. as Christians. But such suffering is one with that of the Old Testament witnesses—the result of obedience to the will of God.

5.13-16. *Salt and light*. In two metaphors, Jesus points to the role of his disciples in the world. 'Light' is an image that was used both of Israel and of the Law in the Old Testament. Now it is the members of the new Israel who are to be a light to the world. Jesus' own mission has already been described in terms of light (*4*.16).

5.17–20. *Jesus and the Law*. These verses emphasize the continuity between the Old Testament and Jesus: his words are the fulfilment of the Old Testament, and do not contradict the Law and the prophets. Verses 18 and 19 are, however, very difficult, for they seem to imply that the Jewish Law in all its details was binding upon members of the Christian community. This attitude seems to contradict what we know from elsewhere of the mind of Jesus, though it may well reflect Matthew's attitude: Jesus himself seems to have been concerned to stress the importance of the spirit, rather than the letter, of the Law, and this is seen in the teaching that follows.

5.21–48. Six antitheses. The teaching of Jesus is here contrasted with that of Moses, with the repeated formula 'You have heard that our forefathers were told . . . But what I tell you is this'. This formula echoes one used in rabbinic teaching on scripture which ran 'Rabbi So-and-So interpreted it thus . . . But I interpret it thus'. Here, however, the contrast is made with the Law of God itself! Part of the Jewish messianic hope was that the Messiah would give Israel a new Law—or rather, that he would truly interpret the old one: clearly, in Matthew's view, this is what Jesus is doing. It will be noted, however, that what Jesus is doing in each case is not to contradict the original commands—rather he sweeps aside all attempts to limit their application, and points to the spirit of the commands. There were other Jewish teachers who interpreted the commandments in a similar, spiritual way; but many of them were engaged in defining their literal meaning accurately, lest there should be accidental breaches—and in so doing, they limited and obscured their true meaning. Cf. similar examples in Mk. *7*.1–23 and *10*.1–9. Jesus refuses to limit the scope of man's responsibility to God, or to place any bounds on what God can demand (cf. Matt. *18*.21 f.).

21–2. Cf, Ex. *20*.13. Jesus points to the root cause of murder—anger, which has been permitted to simmer; he is thus far more radical in his demand than the original commandment. Verses 23–6, though on a related theme, are probably a separate piece of teaching.

27–8. Cf. Ex. *20*.14. Once again, Jesus puts his finger on the cause of adultery, lust. Verses 29–30 seem to be another separate saying, linked here by the common theme of being led astray by what one sees. The same saying appears in Mk. *9*.43–7. By using this strong picture-language, Jesus shocks his listeners into realizing the importance of the choice they make.

31–2. Cf. Deut. *24*.1–4. The other evangelists, in their account of this saying (Mk. *10*.11 f. and Lk. *16*.18) allow no exception, and the phrase about unchastity is probably a later addition to Jesus' original saying. A similar exception is found in another version of the saying in Matt. *19*.9.

80

33–7. Cf. Ex. *20*.7. The Jews had a horror of blaspheming God's name—so great that they never in fact used his name 'Yahweh'. More important, however, is the principle that lies behind the command to fulfil an oath. It is the promise itself which is important, not the form in which it was made.

38–42. Cf. Ex. *21*.24 f. The *lex talionis* was intended to limit revenge, and avoid blood feuds; an eye for an eye was rough justice. Jesus, however, demands that there should be no retaliation, and even that there should be no resistance to insults and unjust demands. To hit someone on the right side of the face—with the back of the hand—was particularly insulting; the 'shirt' or undergarment was sometimes demanded as a legal pledge (cf. Ex. *22*.25–7); compelling someone to go a mile to carry baggage was a custom of the Roman authorities (cf. Matt. *27*.32).

43–8. Cf. Lev. *19*.18. There is no commandment in the Old Testament to hate one's enemies, though in practice, by limiting the definition of 'neighbour' to Israelites, it was assumed that one might hate members of other nations. In the Manual of Discipline (one of the Dead Sea Scrolls), this is in fact made specific: members of the community should 'love everyone whom God has elected, and hate everyone whom he has rejected'. For Jesus, love is not restricted. Those who love become children of God, v. 45, because love is characteristic of him. As God is 'goodness', v. 48 (lit. 'perfect'), so must the disciples be. Cf. Lev. *19*.2: those who belong to God's people must be like him.

6.1–18. *Piety and its reward.* From the interpretation of the Commandments, we turn to sayings about the three traditional activities of Jewish piety—almsgiving, prayer and fasting. The true motive for this must be devotion to God, and not the desire to win praise from men, v. 1. The form of each section is the same: 'When you . . . do not be like the hypocrites . . . I tell you this: they have their reward already. But when you . . . do it in secret; and your Father who sees what is done in secret will reward you' (vv. 2–4, 5–6, 16–18).

2–4. Almsgiving was one of the duties expected of the Jew.

The word translated 'act of charity' in the NEB is from the same Greek root as the word translated 'mercy' in 5.7.

5–6. Private prayer should also be private, not public!

7–15. Other sayings on prayer and on forgiveness. Preachers might take especial note of v. 8, since those conducting public worship often fall into the temptation to treat prayers as an opportunity to give the Almighty a bulletin on the state of his universe! With vv. 9–13, cf. Lk. *11*.2–4. Matthew's is a slightly longer and more formal version, reflecting liturgical use (as do the final phrases added in some manuscripts—see RSV mg.). Luke's 'Father' is a more informal and intimate address. The opening petitions, that God's name (i.e. God himself) should be reverenced, his kingdom come, and his will be done, are synonymous. Only in the second part of the prayer, when the petitioner has aligned himself with the will of God, does he make requests for himself. It is not certain whether the familiar translation 'Give us today our daily bread' is correct, or whether we should read 'bread for tomorrow'—in which case the reference is perhaps to the final messianic feast, and the prayer is a petition to share in the blessings of the Kingdom. 'Wrong' is literally 'debt', and the coming of the Kingdom is of course a time of reckoning. 'The test' is perhaps also to be linked with the coming, Kingdom, since the Jews expected a time of testing to precede it—the activity of the evil one, from whom the disciples should pray to be delivered. Verses 14 f. underline v. 12—cf. also again 5.7.

16–18. Fasting was another duty for the pious Jew, often linked with prayer.

6.19–34. *Single-mindedness.* We seem to have here a collection of sayings, somewhat loosely connected, and found in different contexts in Luke. For Matthew, the link is in the idea of single-mindedness. The command to lay up treasure in heaven (vv. 19–21) sums up the theme of true reward which runs through the previous section. If one's heart is set upon God, and his reward, not upon the praise of men, then one's eye will be sound or healthy—'single' in the older translations, i.e. set upon one target, vv. 22–3. One cannot look in two directions at once—and one cannot serve two masters simultaneously, v. 24: man cannot devote his love and concern to God and to the pursuit of wealth and position and possessions. So they must not centre their lives on material possessions, but on God; the contrast (and the choice) is between God and mammon; between faith and anxious care, vv. 25–34.

7.1–5. *Criticism of others.* The principle of 5.7 is now applied to the specific theme of criticism of others. Verse 6 seems to be a separate saying, and a very difficult one, the exact meaning of which is now lost—as is its relevance to the present context.

7.7–11. *Further teaching about prayer.* God will give the good gifts of the Kingdom to those who ask, and seek and knock.

7.12. *The Golden Rule*—which is a form of the command to love one's neighbour as oneself—sums up all that is demanded in the Hebrew Law about conduct towards others.

7.13–27. *The two ways.* These last sayings in the Sermon all emphasize the contrast between the two ways which lie before men. One way leads to destruction, the other to life (vv. 13 f.; cf. Deut. *30*.15 ff., or Jer *21*.8). The narrow gate leading to life takes up the image of v. 7. Two images are put together in vv. 15–20. The followers of Jesus must not be misled by false prophets, men who appear outwardly to be members of the flock but in fact are wolves—enemies who will ravage the flock; the imagery of sheep and wolves is used in the Old Testament of Israel and her enemies. The way to recognize the wolves is by their fruit! Briars and thistles are unproductive plants (cf. Gn. *3*.18). False discipleship and the failure to bear fruit is also the theme of the saying in vv. 21–3. Though these men acknowledge Jesus as Lord with their lips, he will not acknowledge them at the judgement. The two possibilities are vividly set out in the final parable of the men who built houses on rock and on sand, and who when the test came found they had built, the one wisely, the other foolishly. It is the words of Jesus which must be acted upon—i.e. obeyed—if his hearers are to survive the coming crisis.

28–9. *Conclusion.* The final note by Matthew underlines the importance and authority of Jesus' teaching. 'This discourse' (NEB) is in Greek 'these words'—the same phrase that was used in vv. 24 and 26.

The ministry continued

8.1–4. A leper healed. Matthew uses Mark's story of the cure of a leper (see notes on Mk. *1*.40–5) but omits any reference to Jesus' emotion. As in Mark, the healed man is instructed to obey the regulations laid down in the Law, so that he may be restored to membership of the community. It is notable that this first healing miracle in Matthew tells of an outcast who is made whole, and so recognized once again as a member of Israel.

8.5–13. A Gentile healed. By contrast, the second healing miracle tells of the cure of a Gentile, not simply an outcast from Israel, but a total outsider. Just as Jesus was willing to risk defilement by touching the leper, so he is prepared to do so once again by entering the house of a Gentile, something which no scrupulous Jew would do.

The sick man is, however, healed without being seen by Jesus, because of the remarkable faith of the centurion, which stands in contrast to the disbelief of Israel. No doubt Matthew intends us to understand the distance which separates the sufferer from Jesus as a symbol of the distance which separates the Gentiles from salvation, just as he interprets his cure as pointing to the time when Gentiles will flock into the kingdom and Jews be left in outer darkness (vv. 11–12).

To a modern reader, these two stories seem to be primarily stories about healings. For Matthew, however, they are important primarily becaue they illustrate how particular people—an outcast from Israel and a Gentile—stand in relation to God's salvation, now seen at work in Jesus.

8.14–17. Scripture fulfilled. Once again Matthew uses tradition which is found also in Mark (*1*.29–34). Typically, he rounds off this group of healing stories with a quotation from scripture. This is the only time that Matthew quotes Isa. *53*, and to us it is a very strange use indeed of that passage, since Matthew interprets it of illnesses, not sins, and understands the verbs 'taking' and 'bearing' as meaning 'taking away' and 'bearing off'. What seems to us like an arbitrary use of scripture, however, would have been for Matthew a natural interpretation of a passage promising salvation to those in need.

12.38–42. *Demand for a sign.* Cf. Mk. *8*.11–12, Luke *11*.29–32, Matt. *16*.1–4. This story illustrates well the way in which traditions could be modified and interpreted in different ways. Mark gives us the shortest account, consisting of an abrupt demand from the Pharisees for a sign and a straightforward refusal on the part of Jesus. Matthew has two accounts of the same incident. The first is similar to Mark's version, in that Jesus denounces the present generation, but his reply is considerably expanded with the promise that a sign will indeed be given, namely the sign of Jonah; an explanation of this sign follows. In the second account, in Matt. *16*.1–4, Jesus gives a somewhat different reply,[1] but concludes with the reference to the present generation and the sign of Jonah, for which no explanation is given. In Luke, there is no request for a sign from Pharisees or Sadducees. When the crowds flock to Jesus, he denounces the present generation because it seeks a sign, and declares that the only sign to be given will be that of Jonah, who was a sign to the men of his generation.

It looks very much as if the saying about the sign of Jonah was a puzzle to the evangelists. Luke apparently understood it of Jonah's preaching mission; he was a 'sign' to his contemporaries, in that they repented when he preached to them, but Jesus' own contemporaries have failed to respond to his message, and will therefore be condemned. Matthew, on the other hand, has interpreted the sign in terms of Jonah's deliverance from the great fish; his escape from entombment in the belly of the fish prefigures the resurrection of the Son of

[1] The test is not certain here. Some mss. lack vv. 2–3, and the most likely explanation is that a copyist omitted them accidentally. Alternatively, it is possible that they were not part of the original gospel, but have been added at some stage.

man from the grave after three days and nights. In whatever way this particular saying is interpreted, the point of the story is the failure of those who demand a sign from Jesus to believe the sign which is given them, whether it is in his preaching, his miracles or his resurrection.

16.13–22. *Caesarea Philippi.* This story is almost identical with Mark's account, except that Matthew has added the words addressed by Jesus to Peter in vv. 17–19. It is clear that Matthew has no doubts about the correctness of Peter's 'confession': note how he defines the term 'Christ' in v. 16 in terms of 'the Son of the living God'. Peter's insight into Jesus' identity comes from God himself (cf. *11*.27). According to Matthew it is at this point that Jesus gave Peter (hitherto known as Simon Bar-Jonah) his name; in Mark (*3*.15) and John (*1*.42), however, Jesus gives Peter his new name at an earlier stage in the story. *Peter* comes from a Greek noun *petros,* meaning 'rock', and the equivalent name in Aramaic is *Cephas.* For Matthew, the words of Jesus confirm the significance of Peter's declaration, and the new name which Peter is given underlines the importance of his faith. It is possible that both the renaming of the disciple and the promise that Jesus will found his church upon this rock and give Peter authority over the church originated as post-resurrection sayings (cf. Jesus' command to Peter in Jn. *21*.15–17). If vv. 18–19 came to Matthew as an isolated unit of tradition, he may well have thought the present context a suitable place to set it. By inserting the sayings at this point, Matthew emphasizes the fact that the small group of believing disciples form the kernel of the new community which is to be known as the church.

21.28–22.14. *Three parables.* These three parables, which follow the symbolic action of Jesus in the temple and the destruction of the fig tree, are clearly intended by Matthew to demonstrate Israel's failure. Each of the stories is interpreted allegorically, and in each of them the character or characters representing Israel is contrasted with others who will take the place of Israel.

In the parable of the two sons (*21*.28–31), one son promises to obey his father but fails to do so, while the other at first refuses but repents; the interpretation which follows (vv. 31–2) explains that the outcasts of society ('tax-collectors and harlots') will precede the religious leaders into the kingdom because they have repented.

Matthew's version of the parable of the vineyard (*21*.33–43) is similar to Mark's, but the interpretation is spelt out in v. 43: the kingdom of God will be taken 'from you' and given to others.

The parable of the wedding-feast (*22*.1–10) uses a familiar Jewish image for the future kingdom, since this was sometimes likened to a banquet: but once again, those who should have enjoyed what was prepared for them cut themselves off from taking part in it by their own action, and others take their places. It is clear that Matthew understands this to be a parable about Israel's failure to respond to Jesus, and the subsequent offer of the kingdom to Gentiles. At this point, however, he adds a rider to the story—or perhaps it was originally a separate parable—which is not found in the corresponding passage in Luke (*14*.16–24); it is the story of the wedding-garment (*22*.11–14). The implication seems to be that though the kingdom will be thrown open to outsiders who had not expected a share in it, they too will forfeit their place if they treat the invitation with contempt; those who respond to the invitation must be prepared to accept the obligations which go with it.

23. 1–39. *Judgement on the religious authorities.* This chapter begins with warnings addressed to the crowds and disciples, but soon becomes a series of blistering denunciations pronounced on the religious authorities. A similar passage is found in Lk. *11*.42–52, and a very much shorter one in Mk. *12*.38–40, but Matthew's version is much more bitter than either Mark's or Luke's, and seems out of character with the rest of Jesus' teaching; it appears to reflect the bitter controversies between Christians and Jews which took place during the period when the gospel was in formation. To what extent, then, does this teaching go back to Jesus himself? We have here a good example of the way in which changed circumstances can modify tradition, and so affect the impact which it makes upon its hearers. Sayings which in their present form express bitter denunciation and condemnation may have been adapted from warnings originally given more in sorrow than in anger. Although Jesus certainly opposed Pharisaic teaching in many respects, he was probably a great deal closer to the Pharisees than the gospels suggest, since the split between Judaism and the Church caused bitterness which inevitably affected the retelling of stories about conflicts between Jesus and the religious authorities. Some of the teaching given here echoes that found in chs. 5–7, but it is here presented in a negative form (i.e. condemnation) rather than in the present form used there.

Verses 1–3 repeat the theme of 5.20. In the controversies between Christians and Jews, it is likely that Matthew's community claimed that they were in fact doing what Moses taught more faithfully than the scribes and Pharisees. The behaviour of the Jewish religious leaders described in vv. 5–7 contrasts with that which was required by Jesus in 6.1–18, since they are making a show of religious observances. Phylacteries were small leather boxes containing particular texts from Exodus and Deuteronomy, and they were worn on the forehead and the left arm (Deut. 6.8); fringes or tassels were intended, according to Num. 15.38–40, to remind men of God's commandments. Christian leaders should not look for honour, but should follow the path of service (vv. 8–12; cf. Mk. 10.42–5).

In vv. 13–36 we have a series of seven or eight woes—seven if we omit v. 14, which is missing from the earliest manuscripts. The first, in v. 13, seems to reflect the time at the end of the first century AD when Jewish Christians were pronounced cursed by the religious authorities and expelled from the synagogues. Verse 14 is parallel to the saying found in Mk. 12.40. Verse 15 sugggests considerable Jewish missionary activity, which is confirmed by the many Gentile 'God-fearers' who attended the synagogues (see *Groundwork* 29n); there were not many Gentiles, however, who were prepared to take the further step of becoming a proselyte, that is of accepting circumcision, but those who did may well have been fanatical in their zeal for keeping the Law.

Verses 16–22 condemn casuistry, which enables men to avoid the truth by arguing about the meaning of words. Similarly, those who are condemned in vv. 23–4 are so busy with the minutiae of the Law that they miss the real point of the commandments altogether. The woes in vv. 25–6 and 27–8 both condemn those who are concerned with ceremonial matters, with external appearances rather than inner goodness. The final woe in vv. 29–32 contains a bitter irony: the contemporaries of Jesus honour the prophets of old and denounce those who persecuted them, but in fact they are about to demonstrate that they are no better than those who went before them; they will complete the work of their fathers by killing and crucifying, scourging and persecuting—i.e. by their opposition to Jesus and his followers (vv. 33–44). Judgement is therefore inevitable (vv. 35–6) and the section ends with a lament over Jerusalem, whose fate is now sealed because of the failure of her leaders to respond to Jesus' message.

24.45–25.46. More parables. Mark ends his account of the teaching given by Jesus to four disciples with a parable warning them to be on their guard because the end will come suddenly (Mk. *13*.33–36). Matthew also includes this parable (Matt. *24*.45–51), but he follows it with three more parables on a similar theme.

The story of the ten girls at a wedding (*25*.1–13) is found only in Matthew. The theme is that of being ready to respond to God's summons, and it is clear from the context that Matthew is thinking of the final judgement; probably he interprets the bridegroom in the story as representing Jesus himself, and the problem for the Christian community is the long delay in the return of Jesus (v. 5). It is possible, however, that this verse is an addition to the story; if we take the parable out of the context Matthew has given it and try to think of it in relation to Jesus' ministry, we can see that originally he might have used the story, not to warn his disciples about future events, but to summon his contemporaries to respond to his message here and now. Interpreted in this way, the parable fits into Jesus' challenge to men and women to respond to God's invitation: the time of salvation has arrived, and they are invited to enter, but they must not delay, they must seize the opportunity while it is there. If this was the meaning of the story for those who first heard it, we can see once again how the words of Jesus could be used to speak to men and women in different situations.

The next parable (vv. 14–30) is also interpreted by Matthew as a warning about the final judgement; when the final reckoning comes, those who are faithful will be rewarded, and those who have proved unworthy will be cast into outer darkness. Luke has a somewhat different version of the story in *19*.11–27. For both Matthew and Luke, the parable is a warning about future judgement. But how would the story have sounded when Jesus told it? To his first hearers, it may well have seemed to be a parable about *present* judgement: the time of reckoning has already arrived, in the person of Jesus, and those to whom God has entrusted his gifts are already being called to account. Once again, when it is interpreted within the context of Jesus' ministry, the parable conveys a more urgent message: God's people Israel—and in particular their leaders—stand under judgement already, because of their failure to be good servants.

The final passage in this section, *25*.31–46, is not really a parable at all, but a vivid description of the final judgement. The judge is to be Jesus himself, the Son of man who is now acknowledged as king by those who are brought before him. It is not the Jewish nation which is being judged here, but 'all the nations', i.e. the Gentiles, and the basis of judgement is how they have treated the most insignificant of his brothers; this term is often understood as refering to any human being who is suffering, but it may well be that Matthew interpreted the phrase as meaning a Christian disciple. Disciples are referred to as Jesus' brothers in Matt. *12*.49 and *28*.10, and as 'little ones' in *18*.6, 10, 14 (note that the reference is to those who have faith in Jesus, not to the children with whom they are compared). If Jews are judged by their response to Jesus, the rest of mankind are apparently to be judged by their response to his followers.

27.57–28.20. The resurrection. Matthew's account of the burial of Jesus (*27.57–61*) is similar to that found in Mk. *15.42–7*, but is followed by the story of the setting of a guard at the tomb (*27.62–6*). The story is unlikely to be historical, and probably originated as an answer to Jewish propaganda suggesting that the disciples had stolen the body; the continuation of the story in *28.11–15* depicts this as an explanation deliberately invented by the Jewish authorities to quell the rumours that Jesus had been raised from death.

Matthew expands Mark's account of the visit of the women to the tomb (*28.1–10*). He explains that the stone was rolled away by an angel, who replaces the 'young man' in Mark's account. The women, who in Mark are too frightened to say anything to anyone, in Matthew run to tell the disciples, as they are bidden. For them, the empty tomb proclaims the resurrection. On the way they meet the risen Lord, who repeats the angel's message to the disciples.

The final scene (vv. 16–20) is amazingly abrupt. Jesus meets the eleven disciples and charges them to go into the whole world, making disciples, baptizing and (typical of Matthew) teaching. To a modern reader of the gospel, it seems an unsatisfying resurrection appearance—especially when we read that some of the disciples doubted (v. 17); but this is probably because we are looking for something which Matthew does not intend to provide. We tend to regard resurrection appearances as proofs of the resurrection, but clearly Matthew did not feel the need for these. What he clearly did feel to be necessary was an account of the meeting between Jesus and his disciples, restoring them to the position which they had forfeited through their failure to stand by him, and commissioning them to be his witnesses throughout the world.

Conclusion

Looking at Matthew's gospel as a whole, we see how he

emphasizes the role of Jesus as teacher: in doing so he is no doubt trying to share with his readers his belief that Jesus is superior to Moses, whose teaching lies at the heart of Jewish faith and practice. Not only is Jesus superior to Moses, but his disciples are urged to be more righteous than the most scrupulous observers of the Mosaic Law. It may well be that Matthew wrote his gospel for a community which was under attack from orthodox Jews, and that he was concerned to demonstrate that Christians, far from being blasphemers or law-breakers, were in fact being more faithful to the Law than their opponents; while their Jewish neighbours kept the letter of the Law, they fulfilled its spirit, for they were followers of one who was greater than Moses, and who was himself the fulfilment of both Law and prophets. Commentators often remark on the Jewish character of this gospel; at the same time, however, there is throughout Matthew an emphasis on the failure of Israel. Although Jesus' mission is to Israel alone (*15*.24), Matthew stresses that Israel's failure to respond to the gospel will lead to salvation for others, and he ends with the commission of the risen Jesus to the apostles to preach to the whole world.

Read *Groundwork* 31d–g.

Suggestions for further reading

A. W. Argyle, *St. Matthew* (Cambridge NEB Commentary).
* K. Stendahl on *Matthew* in *Peake's Commentary*, ed. M. Black and H. H. Rowley (Nelson).
* E. Schweizer, *The Good News according to Matthew* (SPCK).
* H. B. Green, *Matthew* (Oxford, New Clarendon Bible).

Chapter 5

The Spirit of the Lord—St. Luke

Passages for special study:

Luke *3*.1–20; *4*.14–30; *5*.1–11; *6*.17–26; *7*.11–23, 36–50;
10; *13*.1–9; *15*; *19*.1–27; *24*.

ONCE again, when we turn to Luke's gospel, we find ourselves
confronted with a mixture of the familiar and the unfamiliar.
The close similarities between Mark and Luke suggest that
Luke has used Mark, but if so he has used only about half of
Mark's material and outline. Some of the non-Markan material which he has included is familiar to us from Matthew,
and some is found only in Luke. Again, some of Luke's stories
are very similar to those which are found in Mark and
Matthew, but are so different in wording that it looks very
much as if, for much of the time, he is using independent
accounts of the same incidents, rather than copying from the
other evangelists. This means that one has to be very careful
how one draws conclusions about the 'changes' which Luke
appears to make to Mark. Commentators have often compared the saying in Mk. *10*.45, e.g., with that found in Lk.
22.27, and concluded that Luke has deliberately omitted the
reference to Jesus' life being given as a ransom. If one looks
more closely at the context of these sayings however (Mk.
10.42 ff. and Lk. *22*.24 ff.), it is easy to see how very different
the two stories are, and it looks as if Luke is using a separate
piece of tradition altogether, not altering Mark.

In order to see the story as Luke is trying to tell it, it is
important once again to read through the whole of his gospel,

and not simply those passages which have been selected for comment here. The following outline will serve as a guide:

Notes on passages for special study

3.1–20 *Message of John.* Both Matthew and Luke expand the account of John the Baptist's teaching which is given by Mark. Notice how Luke, typically, first of all sets the historical scene

(vv. 1–2). Like Mark, Luke quotes from Isa. *40,* but he quotes considerably more of the passage, and the words which he quotes—about mountains being brought low and all mankind seeing God's salvation—are typical of Luke's understanding of the gospel. John's mission is a preparatory one; he calls Israel to repent because of the coming judgement. Repentance, however, must be genuine. It is no use relying on the fact that one belongs to the chosen people, and assuming that one will therefore share in God's salvation. Only Luke gives us a sample of John's teaching, spelling out what he understands by 'fruits of repentance'. Both Matthew and Luke emphasize the theme of judgement much more than Mark: cf. Lk. *3.*7–9 with Matt. *3.*7–10 and the final saying in Lk. *3.*16 f. and Matt. *3.*11 f. with Mk. *1.*7 f. In Mark, John simply contrasts his own baptism in water with the Coming One's baptism in Spirit, but in the other gospels John speaks of future judgement: those who are not baptized now with water will be baptized with fire hereafter! It looks as if Matthew and Luke have both made use of another account of John's teaching at this point, in preference to that given by Mark.

*4.*14–15. *Jesus preaches in synagogues.* Like Mark (*1.*14 f.), Luke begins his account of Jesus' ministry by describing how he taught in Galilee. It is typical of these early chapters of Luke that he emphasizes that Jesus came 'in the power of the Spirit'. He has already described the descent of the Spirit in *3.*22, and told us that Jesus returned from the Jordan 'full of the Holy Spirit' and was then 'led by the Spirit' in the wilderness (*4.*1 f.). This theme is spelt out in the next section.

*4.*16–30. *Jesus preaches in Nazareth.* The message of Jesus' sermon is the fulfilment of scripture: the promises of Isa. *61* are now fulfilled in his ministry. Readers of the gospel already know that the Spirit of the Lord is upon Jesus, and that he has been anointed by God for a specific task. These words from Isa. *61* spell out that task, and serve as a manifesto of Jesus' future ministry. From now on, Luke will show us how this scripture is fulfilled, as Jesus preaches good news (*4.*43 f.), sets men and women free from disease and demons (*4.*33–41,

5.12–26, *6*,6–10), raises the dead (7.11–17). heals the blind (7.21), proclaims the day of salvation (*6*.20–3). Initial reaction to Jesus's words is favourable (cf. *2*.52, *4*,15), but the incident ends with an attempt on the part of the congregation to lynch the preacher—an ominous reminder that Jesus will ultimately be rejected by his own people. The sayings in vv. 23–8 seem more appropriate *after* this rejection than as its cause; certainly the reference to Jesus' miracles at Capernaum in v. 23 seems to belong to a later stage in the ministry, since Luke does not record a visit to Capernaum until v. 31. The stories about the help which the great prophets Elijah and Elisha gave to non-Israelites are interpreted as pointers to what happens in the ministry of Jesus: salvation comes to Gentiles, rather than to those who belong to God's people. Yet it is not because Jesus does not offer them salvation. He proclaims the good news to his own people, and his own people reject him.

5.1–11. The large catch of fish. This story is not found in Mark and Matthew, but a similar story is told of the risen Jesus in Jn. *21*.1–8, where it leads up to the conversation between Jesus and Peter, in which Peter is commanded to feed the Lord's sheep. Here, the theme of discipleship is linked directly with the story. Simon Peter, James and John are called to be fishers of men (cf. Mk. *1*.17); the large catch of fish symbolizes the future work of the Church. However unworthy they may feel, Jesus has need of them .The call of Jesus is instantly obeyed, and the men leave everything to follow Jesus. 'Everything' seems to mean a prosperous fishing business (cf. Mk. *10*.28).

6.17–26. Beatitudes and woes. Compare Luke's four beatitudes with Matthew's nine (Matt. *5*.3–10), and notice how Luke has balanced his beautitudes with four woes. It is difficult to know which version is closer to the words of Jesus himself. Probably both forms have been used and adapted as they have been handed on. Notice how the four beatitudes which Luke has selected, together with the four woes, are all linked with the theme of reversal. Those who are poor and hungry and sorrowful and persecuted now will receive a reward in the future, whereas those who are rich and full, happy and honoured at present will lose all that they have. The beatitudes offer reassurance to the disciples, while the woes warn those who are complacent. Luke's version of the beatitudes seems materialistic, but he points to the truth that in God's eyes the values of this world are reversed.

7.11–17. *A widow's son is raised.* This story is similar to stories told about Elijah and Elisha (1 Kgs. *17*.17–24; 2 Kgs. *4*.18–37), and it is therefore not surprising that the crowd is said to respond by declaring: 'A great prophet has arisen among us!' Jesus had compassion on the woman; not only had she lost both her husband and her son, but she was deprived thereby of material support.

7.18–23. *The message to John.* It is often suggested that this story indicates that John the Baptist, after his imprisonment, began to lose faith in Jesus and to wonder whether or not he had been right to believe that Jesus was the Messiah. It is important, however, to read the story as Luke tells it. Although Luke describes a meeting between the mothers of John and Jesus, he does not tell us that John and Jesus themselves ever met, apart from the occasion of Jesus' baptism. Even that can hardly be described as a meeting: Luke simply records that Jesus was baptised (*3*.21). There is no suggestion that John recognized Jesus then as the one who was to follow him, or that he shared the experience recorded in *3*.22. Both Matthew (*3*.14–17) and John (*1*.29–34) tell us that John did in fact recognize Jesus as the one about whom he had spoken, but it is easy to understand how this tradition would have developed; Christians would assume that John realized from the first who Jesus was. The account given in Mark and Luke, in which John did not recognize Jesus, is more likely to be historical. If so, then this story in Lk. 7 reflects hope rather than despair; it is not that John is doubting whether Jesus is, after all, the Coming One, but rather that he is wondering, from the rumours that have reached him, whether his message is at last being fulfilled. The answer Jesus gives is not merely a verbal one, for the messengers see him at work for themselves, curing the sick and demon-possessed, and giving sight to the blind. Notice how the message to John not only sums up the activity of Jesus in the last few chapters, but echoes the words quoted from Isa. *61* in *4*.18 f.

7.36–50. *A sinful woman finds forgiveness.* All four gospels tell the story of a woman who anoints Jesus with perfume (either his head, Mark and Matthew, or his feet, Luke and John), but in the other three it comes as part of the passion narrative, and the story is linked with Jesus' death. Luke's story is quite different: the woman is said to be a sinner, and her action demonstrates her repentance and gratitude. Whereas the righteous Pharisee failed to offer Jesus simple courtesies, she paid him the honour appropriate to a distinguished guest. The point of the story, that the sinner finds forgiveness, is similar to the parable of the Pharisee and the tax collector in Lk. *18*.10–15; in each case, the Pharisee condemns the 'sinner', and in doing so demonstrates his own shortcoming.

10.1–16. *Seventy disciples sent out.* In *9*.1–6, Luke recorded the sending out of the twelve; now the mission of Jesus is extended, as more disciples are sent out. The number 70 (perhaps 72—the textual evidence is uncertain) may be a deliberate echo of the 70 elders (or 72, including Eldad and Medad) appointed to help Moses lead Israel (Num. *11*.16–30); like Moses, Jesus needs men to help him in his mission. Some commentators suggest that the 70 represent the 70 nations of the world, but they are not in fact sent beyond the borders of Israel; the mission to the Gentiles comes later. The disciples are to travel light, and they are not to tarry by the way, for their mission is urgent. It is also of vital importance: those who receive them will be close to the kingdom of God, but those who reject their message will be condemned on the day of judgement. The authority which Jesus gives to his disciples means that those who reject them reject him, and those who reject him reject the call of God himself.

101

10.17–24. *Jesus rejoices at Satan's defeat.* The defeat of the demons is no isolated event; it is symbolic of the downfall of Satan, whose power crumbles before the in-breaking Kingdom of God. Jesus praises God because what is happening in his ministry is being shared by simple people, even though the religious leaders fail to grasp its significance. The saying in v. 22 and its parallel in Matt. *11*.27 is quite unlike any other in the synoptics, and reminds one of the Fourth gospel. It expresses the special status of Jesus as Son, and his role as revealer of the Father. The position which had once belonged to Israel, of being in a special relationship with God, and making all his will known to mankind, has now been taken over by Jesus.

10.25–37. *Loving one's neighbour.* The parable of the Good Samaritan is found only in Luke. The lawyer's summary of the Law is attributed in Mk. *12*.28 ff. to Jesus himself. The question 'And who is my neighbour?' is typical of the legalistic attitude which Jesus condemns. It springs from the man's desire to justify himself; he wishes to define his duty by defining his neighbour, so that he can say that he has done all that is required of him. Jesus' reply, by contrast, points to an attitude which does not set up barriers or draw up definitions: even those whom one would normally label enemies are included in Jesus' understanding of the term 'neighbour', since it means anyone who needs one's love. Instead of *defining* 'neighbour' he explains what is means to *be* a neighbour, since there are no limits to those whom one must treat as neighbours. Jesus' story no doubt startled his hearers: after the priest and the Levite they would perhaps expect to hear of an ordinary Israelite layman—certainly not of a Samaritan! They would have been shocked by the idea that a hated Samaritan might be the hero of the story. His generous behaviour stands in stark contrast to that of the two religious leaders, who 'passed by on the other side' of the road through fear that they might be contaminated by what looked like a corpse, and so prevented from worshipping God in the temple!

10.38–42. *Mary and Martha.* This story is found only in Luke,

102

although Mary and Martha appear also in Jn. *11* and *12*. It might seem strange that Jesus apparently rebuked Martha for her concern in looking after her guests; like the Samaritan in the parable, she was showing generosity in a very practical way. The point of the story, however, is to underline the importance of Jesus' teaching: the response which his hearers made to him took priority over everything else.

13.1–9. *Future judgement*. In a longer section on the theme of future judgement (*12*.35–*13*.9), Luke includes some teaching which is not found in the other gospels. Verses 1–5 warn his hearers against complacency. Some of them make the mistake of assuming that disasters are a demonstration of God's wrath, picking out the 'sinners' from the righteous. But God's judgement does not work in this way. The disasters which have come to some should be seen, rather, as a warning of what the final reckoning will mean. The parable of the fig tree, vv. 6–9, reminds us of the 'acted parable' of the fig tree in Mk. *11*.12–14, 20–1, and it is possible that what was originally a story told by Jesus has been changed, in the Marcan tradition, into a story about Jesus. Although both stories are about judgement, however, the emphasis in Luke's version is somewhat different: the tree is under sentence of death—yet it is given one last chance to bear fruit before it is cut down.

15.1–32. *Three parables*. The parable of the lost sheep occurs in Matthew (*18*.12–14), but the other two parables are found only in Luke. Notice how the setting which is given to a parable affects the meaning. In Matthew, the parable is addressed to the disciples, and clearly Matthew has understood it as a warning to the future leaders of the church to care for the members of their flock. In Luke however, the story is told by Jesus when the religious leaders complain about him mixing with 'sinners'. Jesus justifies his behaviour by telling three stories which demonstrate the joy experienced by men and women when what has been lost is found: how much greater is the joy of God when sinners repent. It seems likely that Luke's setting is closer to the original. The third parable,

vv. 11 ff., takes the form of a story. The division of the property in v. 12 seems strange to us, but similar customs are recorded in some eastern countries. The fact that the younger son ends up feeding the pigs shows how low he has fallen, since pigs were regarded as unclean animals by Jews. Verses 25–32 introduce a new theme—the resentment of the elder brother. It is easy to see the parallel between his attitude, in refusing to join in the celebrations, and that of the Pharisees, who raise objections when 'sinners' respond to Jesus' preaching.

19.1–10. *Zacchaeus finds salvation.* Once again, Luke tells a story about Jesus welcoming the company of someone who was regarded as an outcast of society. As a chief tax collector, Zacchaeus was an agent of the hated Romans, and so treated as an outsider. Moreover, his position enabled him to extract far more than the required tax from his countrymen, and to pocket the surplus. His response to Jesus is immediate and generous, and by his action he demonstrates his repentance for his past behaviour: he is therefore no longer an outcast from Israel, but a true son of Abraham. The final saying, in v. 10, reminds us of Mk. *10*.45, but the imagery is close to that of Lk. *15*.3–7.

19.11–27. *The parable of the pounds.* In Matthew's version of this story (*25*.14–30), three servants are entrusted with different amounts. Luke's version is somewhat different, but the reactions of the servants are similar. Although Jesus may have used the parable to impress upon his hearers the need to take urgent action, because the time of reckoning was at hand, Luke has used it to teach his readers that the kingdom of God is not to be expected immediately (v. 11). One day, the Son of man will return, having received the kingly power, like the nobleman in the story (v. 15); in the meanwhile, Christians are entrusted with certain duties, like the ten servants, each of whom was given a pound. On the day of reckoning, the servants will be called to account, and will be rewarded or punished according to their response; as for the enemies of the king (vv. 14, 27), they will be slain. It is easy to see, by comparing Matthew and Luke, how extra details have crept into the story and been allegorized, as it was applied to the situation of the early Christians.

The passion and resurrection

The significant feature of Luke's passion narrative is that for much of the time he seems to be using independent tradition unknown to the other evangelists, even though he continues to make use of Marcan material. The most notable differences are seen in the following passages, which are found in Luke but not in Mark:

22.15–17 Saying over the cup. There is a textual problem in Luke's account of the Last Supper. According to some mss., Jesus gave the disciples another cup, after the bread; other mss., omit this reference to a second cup. If the shorter text is original, then presumably the reference to the second cup has been added to bring Luke into line with the other gospels. This suggests that the form of the liturgy was by no means fixed when Luke was writing. If the longer text is original, then presumably a puzzled scribe omitted the reference to one of the two cups, but somewhat strangely omitted the second, not the first.

22.31–3 Saying to Simon about Satan
35–8 Saying about swords
43–4 Jesus' agony
23.4–16 Trial before Herod
27–32 Lament for Jerusalem
39–43 The two bandits
55–6 Women watch the burial

24.1–12. *Women at the tomb.* Like Mark, Luke tells the story of the women who come to anoint Jesus' body and find an empty tomb. Instead of Mark's young man in white, Luke has two men in dazzling apparel, who ask why they look for the living among the dead. Although the women are frightened, they are not struck dumb, as in Mark, but manage to convey the message to the disciples. It may seem remarkable that all four gospels begin the story of the resurrection with the visit of women to the tomb, since the witness of women was unlikely to count for much in Jewish society; their words were likely to be dismissed as an idle tale (v. 11). Yet in the natural course of events, it would be women who came to anoint the dead body. In the Fourth gospel, Peter and another disciple are said to have visited the tomb, and some manuscripts have added a reference to Peter doing so here in v. 12.

24.13–35. The road to Emmaus. This story is found only in Luke. It is interesting to note that he records this first resurrection appearance as an experience shared by two disciples who were not included among the Twelve. Their failure to recognize Jesus suggests that his resurrection body was understood to be different in some way to his previous appearance. It is only when he breaks the bread and blesses it that they recognize him. It is significant that several of the resurrection stories are linked with the theme of Jesus sharing a meal with his disciples (see also v. 42; John *21*.12 f.). One of the features of the early Christian community was to eat together, and the meal was understood as a means of fellowship with the risen Christ, as well as with other Christians (cf. Acts *2*.46; 1 Cor. *10*.14–22). Verses. 26 f. describe the risen Christ himself spelling out the meaning of the Jewish scriptures: rightly understood, they all point forward to his sufferings and vindication. However it happened, there is no doubt that after the resurrection, the disciples came to interpret the scriptures in a new light, and to see in them meanings which had previously not been apparent to them. The question in v. 26 sums up Luke's understanding of Jesus' death and vindication: it was necessary—because it was part of God's plan—that the Christ should suffer, and enter into his glory through death. As soon as the two disciples recognize Jesus, he vanishes: clearly Luke is not thinking here of Jesus' body in a materialistic way.

It is strange that none of the gospels contain an account of the Lord's appearance to Simon (v. 34; cf. 1 Cor. *15*.5).

24.36–49. *Jesus appears to the disciples.* This time, Jesus appears suddenly: clearly his body is not an ordinary physical one. But Luke is concerned to stress that he is not a ghost: the disciples can see Jesus and recognize him, they can touch him and feel that he is alive; finally he asks for food and eats it. It is impossible for us now to sort out these apparently contradictory statements; we cannot explain how anybody could both appear and vanish, and yet have physical substance. It is more important, however, to try to understand the significance of the stories as they are told. What is being conveyed is an overwhelming awareness of the presence of the risen Christ—an awareness which was experienced especially when his followers met and ate together; the stories emphasize the reality of his presence, and convey at one and the same time both a sense of continuity between Jesus of Nazareth and the risen Christ, and a sense of otherness.

Once again, Luke emphasizes the way in which the resurrection enabled the disciples to read scripture in a new light (vv. 44–6). The final words of the risen Christ to his disciples (vv. 47–9) set out the mission which he is entrusting to them. They are to preach repentance and forgiveness in Christ's name, beginning from Jerusalem. They have been the witnesses of all that has happened, and in order to equip them for their task, he will send the promise of his Father upon them—i.e., the Holy Spirit. These themes are repeated in Acts *1*.6–8, where Luke gives another account of this final meeting of Jesus with the disciples.

24.50–3. *Jesus leaves the disciples.* These verses, also, have a parallel in Acts, namely in *1*.9–11. Luke seems to have two versions of the same story, and he binds his two volumes together by ending the first and beginning the second with an account of the ascension. It does not seem to worry him that one account is placed on Easter day, the other after forty days have passed. It is, of course, possible that we should omit the phrase 'and was carried up into heaven', but the great majority of manuscripts contain this phrase, and it looks as if it was omitted in an attempt to sort out the discrepancy between this story and Acts 1.

107

The gospel ends where it began, in the temple at Jerusalem. It is from there that the disciples will begin their mission to the world (v. 47; cf. Acts *1*.8).

Read *Groundwork* 31 h–k and 30.

Suggestions for further reading

G. B. Caird, *St. Luke* (Penguin).

G. W. H. Lampe on *Luke* in *Peake's Commentary*.

E. E. Ellis, *The Gospel of Luke* (New Century Bible, Oliphants).

C. H. Dodd, *Parables of the Kingdom* (Fontana).

J. Jeremias, *Rediscovering the Parables* (SCM).

D. van Daalen, *The Real Resurrection* (Collins).

Chapter 6

The Gospel for all nations—Acts

Passages for special study:

Acts *1–4*; *6*; *7*.44–60; *8*.1–8, 14–17, 26–40; *9–11*; *12*.1–4; *13*; *15*.

WE have seen that Mark, when he came to write his gospel, was almost certainly doing something entirely new. When Matthew and Luke came to write their gospels, they had a model on which to base their books. Turning to Acts, we find that it is Luke who is the innovator—and as far as we know, he had no imitators. There are no Synoptic Acts—and any student who has wrestled with the Synoptic gospels probably feels grateful that this is so! The fact that Luke has the field to himself can, however, be misleading. With only one account of events in Jerusalem during the first days of the Church, and only Luke's version of Paul's missionary work, we are inclined to think that everything is plain sailing. But if Mark, Matthew and John had all written second volumes, might they not have produced somewhat different pictures? One can imagine that their accounts of the Church's life and witness would have been even more varied than their presentations of the gospel.

There is, in fact, one area where we do meet the kind of problem which sometimes confronts us in the gospels, when two authors give different accounts of the same event, or interpret it differently. This is in what Luke has to say about Paul. More than half of Luke's second volume is taken up with the story of Paul. For much of this material there is no

109

parallel anywhere, for Luke's concern is to tell a story, and Paul's is to write pastoral letters to his churches, but sometimes we are able to compare what Luke says with something in one of Paul's letters. The problem is that where we can compare the two, the pictures rarely fit together easily; it is notoriously difficult, for example, to fit together Paul's own account of his visits to Jerusalem with that given by Luke. And when Luke gives an account of one of Paul's sermons, it does not sound very much like the Paul we know from the letters!

The reason for this difficulty is, of course, that we have too little information to produce a 'history of the early Church' or a 'life of St. Paul', and it is therefore foolish to try to construct these out of the material which we have. Just as Luke was writing a theological tract in his gospel, so also he planned Acts, the continuation of his story, as an exercise in propaganda. If he chose his material carefully in volume 1, we can expect him to do the same in volume 2. Although Paul was for him clearly the key figure in his story, he was not writing a life of Paul, and therefore will not necessarily have told us everything he knew about Paul's travels and tribulations. Indeed, he does not even tell us about Paul's death. Luke has picked out those stories which are relevant to his purpose.

What, then, was his purpose? Many different explanations have been given, but basic to his purpose seems to have been the desire to show that Christian faith is the true fulfilment of Judaism, and that the Gentile mission is the true role of Christianity. In the gospel, he showed how the story of God's activity recorded in the Old Testament continued in the person and work of Jesus. Now he shows how this continues in the apostles, and in the Church of which they formed the nucleus. In obedience to the command of the risen Jesus (*1*.8), this church expands outwards from its centre in Jerusalem, going further and further afield—through Judea and Samaria, and finally to the ends of the earth. Luke demonstrates that the events which he describes are the work of God, and that the Christian community is God's people, by showing us, first, how Old Testament texts are fulfilled in Jesus (e.g. *2*.17 ff., 25 ff., 34; *8*.32 f.), and, secondly how the

110

Holy Spirit legitimizes each step as it is taken (e.g. *2*.4; *8*.29; *10*.19, 44; *13*.2).

Luke begins his story in Jerusalem in the weeks following the resurrection. It is tempting to suppose that the picture he gives us of the early Christian community is an accurate one, but we need to remember that Luke is writing many years later. Inevitably, anyone looking back on this early period will see it in the light of later experiences, just as those looking back on the ministry of Jesus saw it in the light of the resurrection. It is difficult for any of us to remember what we felt like years ago, or to trace precisely how our beliefs have changed as our experience has been enlarged. We must beware, then, of taking these early chapters as an exact account of what the beliefs of the earliest Christian community were. They may well reflect the way in which Christians understood their faith at a later period.

Read *Groundwork* 29 and 34.

Notes on passages for special study

1.1–14. *The ascension.* Only Luke describes the ascension as a separate event taking place some time after the resurrection, and we have seen that in his gospel he seems to know a tradition similar to that used by Matthew, linking the ascension much more closely to the resurrection. This discrepancy need not worry us, if we remember that to speak of Christ's ascension is primarily to make a statement of theological truth: Jesus has not only been raised from the dead, he has been exalted to the right hand of God. The image is that of an eastern court, where the man sitting at the monarch's right hand is the most important in the land. In other words, Jesus is not only alive, but now exercises authority and power. Paul, who writes sometimes of Christ's resurrection and sometimes of his exaltation as Lord, does not seem to distinguish between these as two events. In describing the ascension as taking place after forty days (i.e. after a fairly long period of time), Luke is giving his explanation of the change between the period during which the risen Lord appeared to the disciples and the present, when he is known to the Church through the Spirit.

The words of Jesus pick up the prophecy of John the Baptist, and point forward to Pentecost (*1*.5): if the disciples are to continue the mission of Jesus, they need the power of the Holy Spirit. Compare with this story the account of Elijah's ascension into heaven (2 Kgs. *2*.1–15). Elisha asks for a double share of Elijah's spirit. A double share of the property is the inheritance of the eldest son, so Elisha is really asking to be Elijah's true successor; the fact that he carries on Elijah's work, speaking fearlessly and performing similar miracles, is a demonstration that 'the spirit of Elijah rests on Elisha'. In Acts, we shall find the disciples carrying on the work of Jesus, preaching and performing miracles, in the power of the Spirit which he promised them.

Even now, however, the disciples have not really grasped what the mission entrusted to them is, and are thinking of the kingdom of God in political terms (*1*.6). But the time of the end is still unknown (*1*.7); meanwhile, the disciples have a commission to carry out, and must not stand gazing into heaven (*1*.11). So the disciples return to Jerusalem, as they have been commanded (*1*.12–14).

1.15–26. *The election of Matthias.* The treachery and death of Judas meant that the group of twelve disciples chosen to represent Israel (as its twelve new 'patriarchs') had been reduced to eleven. Hence the need to choose a replacement from the larger number of disciples who had been followers of Jesus, and had been witnesses of his resurrection. The casting of lots was at that time a normal way of seeking divine guidance. There is no suggestion in any of our sources that anyone other than Judas was replaced when he died. The twelve formed a unique group, and it was because of his treachery, not his death, that Judas forfeited his place (*1*.20).

2.1–3. *The gift of the Spirit.* Pentecost (which fell fifty days after Passover) was the Jewish festival celebrating the completion of the cereal harvest (cf. Deut. *16*.9–12). It was also associated with the offering of first-fruits, and was therefore

112

a fitting occasion for the gift of the Holy Spirit—described later by St. Paul as 'first-fruits' (Rom. 8.23) and a pledge of things to come (2 Cor. 1.22; 5.5). Pentecost was also the time when the Jews celebrated the giving of the Law to Moses. For the early Christian community, life in the Spirit came to replace life according to the Law; God's will was no longer revealed in the Torah, but in the experience of the living Christ, through the Spirit.

The images which Luke uses to describe the event—a mighty wind and tongues of fire—attempt to convey the tremendous sense of power and of the presence of God experienced on this occasion: 'they were all filled with the Holy Spirit'.

The first demonstration of this new force in the disciples' lives was, according to Luke, the gift of tongues, enabling them to proclaim the gospel to all nations. The phenomenon which Luke describes here is quite different from what Paul refers to as the gift of tongues in 1 Cor. 14. According to Luke, the disciples 'began to speak in other tongues', and everyone present 'heard them speaking in their own language'—a phenomenon which reminds one of the instantaneous translation service provided at a modern international conference. According to Paul, however, certain Christians were inspired to speak on occasion in tongues, and unless an interpreter was present, the rest of the congregation was unable to understand what was said.

Either we must suppose that Luke and Paul are describing two different phenomena, or we must conclude that Luke is giving his own understanding of a tradition which has come down to him, that the disciples spoke in tongues—i.e. uttered ecstatic speech. If the disciples uttered ecstatic speech of the kind described by Paul, the crowd might well have been bewildered (1.6), and some would have concluded that the disciples were drunk (1.13). In fact there would have been no need to speak in 'other languages' to this cosmopolitan crowd, for they would all have understood either Aramaic or Greek. There was, however, a Jewish tradition that on Sinai the angels proclaimed the Law to all the nations of the world in their own languages, though only Israel undertook to obey

113

it. If Luke knew this tradition, he would certainly think it appropriate if now the disciples proclaimed 'the mighty works of God' (*1*.11) to men from every nation. This proclamation of the gospel at Pentecost foreshadows the rest of Luke's story. Jews from every part of the known world heard the gospel in their own language. In other words, although the hearers are all Jews, the mission of the Church to the world has already begun.

1.14–41. *Peter's Pentecost sermon.* Empowered by the Holy Spirit, Peter now addresses the crowd. We can hardly expect anyone to have remembered exactly what Peter said by the time Luke came to write this report, many years later. The style of the sermon is the same as the rest of Acts, and clearly it has been written by Luke. What we do not know, however, is whether Luke is using some kind of source—i.e. someone's recollection of what he heard Peter say on this occasion—or whether Luke is writing what he thinks would have been an appropriate sermon for Peter to have delivered. It was normal practice at that time for historians to write what they considered appropriate speeches for the men whose exploits they were describing—much as Shakespeare wrote appropriate speeches for the characters in his historical plays. If Luke has followed this practice, then clearly we must treat 'Peter's' sermon as evidence for Luke's understanding of the gospel, not for Peter's. Even if Luke was using a source, we must remember that we do not know how accurate this was or to what extent Peter's original words had been interpreted in the light of later Christian experience. We must beware, then, of assuming that these speeches in Acts give us a summary of the very earliest Christian preaching.

This first sermon begins with a long quotation from Joel, the significance of which is that the time of salvation has arrived (cf. Jesus' first sermon in Lk. *4*. 16 ff.). The proof of this is the outpouring of the Spirit.

But the coming of the Spirit is only the last in a series of events. The central theme of this sermon is that what has happened in the life, ministry, death and resurrection of Jesus is all part of God's plan and purpose. That this is so was

114

demonstrated during the ministry by the 'mighty works and wonders and signs' which God did through him (v. 22), and has been confirmed by the fact that God raised him from the dead, an event to which the disciples can testify (v. 32). The outpouring of the Spirit is a sign of his exaltation to God's right hand (v. 33), the proof that God has installed him as Lord and Christ (v. 36).

Further confirmation that this was all part of God's plan is seen in the fact that scripture has been fulfilled. The outpouring of the Spirit is the fulfilment of Joel 2.28–32, and a sign that the time of salvation has come. The resurrection of Jesus fulfils Ps. *16*.8–11, and his exaltation Ps. *110*.1. The argument used here in quoting the psalms assumes that they were written by David: since they were not fulfilled in relation to David himself, they must be understood as prophecies regarding his descendant, the future Messiah. Modern scholars think it unlikely that these psalms were composed by David: in any case, they were intended to describe past events, not to prophesy future ones. Ps. *16* is a thanksgiving for God's salvation of the righteous; Ps. *110* describes the victory of the nation's king over other kings. In the light of this knowledge, we cannot today use these quotations in the way in which they are used here. Nevertheless, Christians will still want to argue that the confidence in God expressed by the Psalmist (whoever he was) was 'fulfilled' in Jesus; the quotation from Ps. *16* is an appropriate summary of Jesus' trust in God, and the words from Ps. *110* are an equally appropriate way of expressing the Church's faith in Christ's exaltation.

The response of the people is immediate. Peter calls on them to 'Repent and be baptized' (v. 38), much as John the Baptist had done. Now, however, they are to be baptized in the name of Jesus; moreover, they are to be baptized with the Spirit, as well as with water.

2.41–47. The Christian community. According to this picture, Jewish Christians continued to worship in the temple, since they saw their new faith as the fulfilment of the Jewish religion; but they also met together in one another's homes as groups of Christians. This pattern probably continued for some time, though outside Jerusalem, Christians would have attended their local synagogues. Christian worship was centred on a·fellowship meal (vv. 42, 46).

3.1–10. A lame man healed. Peter and John are on the way to pray in the temple—they, too, are faithful Jews—when they see a lame man asking for alms. Without hesitation, Peter heals him—in the name of Jesus: the work which Jesus began is continued by his disciples.

3.11–26. Peter's second sermon. This theme is stressed in the sermon which follows: what the disciples do, they do through the power of Jesus (vv. 12, 16). The sermon describes the death of Jesus (for which Peter's audience are in part responsible, vv. 13–15, 17), and his resurrection (of which the disciples are witnesses, v. 15).Once again, it is emphasized that all this has taken place in fulfilment of scripture (vv. 18, 21–5), and once again the message is 'Repent!' (v. 19). A new note is introduced into the message with the reference to the future coming of God's anointed (or Christ), namely Jesus, who has been received into heaven until the time appointed (vv. 20 f.; cf. *1*.11).

Notice the names which are used for Jesus in this chapter. 'Christ' (vv. 18, 20) is familiar enough. More unusual are 'God's servant' (vv. 13, 26), 'the Holy and Righteous One' (v. 14), 'the Author of Life' (v. 15) and 'a prophet like Moses' (v. 22). The first Christians used a great variety of Old Testament terms and expressions to try to convey what their faith in Jesus meant, and some of these proved more useful than others. Those used here are appropriate terms for Peter to use in addressing Jews, and for Luke to use in stressing the theme of the fulfilment of scripture. Both Moses and David were referred to as God's 'servant'; now the term is used of Jesus, who is shown here to be the successor of Moses, just as in ch. *2* he was seen to be the descendant of David. Commentators sometimes trace the term to the so-called 'Servant Songs' of Deutero-Isaiah, but there is no evidence to suggest that those passages are of particular importance here.

4.1–31. *Before the Sanhedrin.* Already Peter and John, like Jesus before them, were in trouble with the religious authorities. The Sadducees' annoyance stemmed from the fact that the disciples were preaching the resurrection of Jesus, and the Sadducees rejected even the belief in a future resurrection held by the Pharisees. Peter's defence is made in the power of the Holy Spirit—cf. the promise of Lk. *12*.11 f. It stresses once again that what the disciples do is done in the power of Jesus. It is addressed to the Sanhedrin—hence the words 'whom you crucified'. Ps. *118*.22 was an important proof-text of the rejection and vindication of Jesus for the early Church: we have met it once already in Mk. *12*.10. The authorities are unable to deny that a notable sign has been performed, and their attempt to silence the disciples is ineffectual. The prayer of the Church, following their release, does not at first seem particularly appropriate, since it quotes Ps. *2*.1 f., and interprets it of the opposition of both Gentiles and Jews to Jesus. The point must be that even this was part of God's plan (v. 28); now the disciples are under a similar attack. Hence their prayer for boldness (v. 29, cf. vv. 13 and 31). Notice that both David and Jesus are referred to as God's 'servant', a term of honour (vv. 25, 27, 30); the word used for the disciples in v. 29 is normally translated 'slaves'. Verse 31 echoes the Pentecost experience.

4.32–7. *The Christian community.* Once again, as in Acts *2*, the Spirit's presence is seen in the disciples' fearless proclamation of the gospel and the community's life of fellowship. The sharing of property is a sign of this fellowship. This is why the attempt to deceive the Christian community by witholding property is seen as a sin against the Spirit (*5*.1–11).

Acts *5* continues the themes of the growth of the Christian community, the 'signs and wonders' performed by the apostles, and the inability of the authorities to silence them: even imprisonment does not stop them teaching 'in the name of Jesus'. The words of Gamaliel in vv. 38 f. show us how Luke wishes his readers to interpret this evidence.

6.1–7. *Appointment of the seven.* As the Church grew, tension

117

arose between two groups: the Hellenists (an unusual word which seems to mean Greek-speaking Jews) and the Hebrews (i.e. those Jews who spoke Aramaic). The former would be Jews from the 'Dispersion' (i.e. who had previously lived outside Palestine) who were now resident in Jerusalem. The two groups probably differed in outlook as well as in language. The Hellenists were probably less strict than the Hebrews in their devotion to the Law and the temple. According to Luke, the dispute between the two groups was concerned with the daily distribution to those who were in need: the reference to widows suggests that this was a kind of poor relief, rather than an experiment in communal living. The decision to appoint seven men to deal with this situation is reminiscent of Num. *11*.1–24, where Moses appoints seventy elders to help him deal with the complaints of the people about food. The seven men are chosen 'to serve tables', and it is the Greek word for 'serve' which has given us the term 'deacon' by which they have come to be known. The strange thing about Luke's story, however, is that in the chapters which follow, these seven men are not described as dealing with administration at all, and at least two of them seem to be quite as busy with the 'ministry of the word' as the apostles! Moreover, the men chosen all have Greek names, which seems strange if they were appointed to see fair play in a mixed community. Possibly we have here a list of men chosen to be evangelists in the Greek-speaking Jewish community, and Luke was mistaken in thinking that they were appointed to deal with problems of administration. In Jewish thought, the laying-on of hands symbolized 'solidarity' between persons; in this case, it seems to indicate that the apostles imparted to the seven deacons a share in their mission, spiritual gifts and authority.

6.8–15. Stephen. The work of Stephen is described in terms parallel to those used of the apostles (vv. 8, 10). He seems to have preached in the synagogues attended by Dispersion Jews, and soon found himself in trouble. He was accused before the Sanhedrin of blasphemous attacks on the Law and the temple. The accusations by false witnesses remind us of those brought against Jesus (cf. Mk. *14.55*–9): those who follow Jesus are already sharing his fate.

The very long speech of Stephen in ch. *7* is certainly no defence against the charges brought against him. Verses 1–43 are an account of Israel's history, showing how the people had again and again resisted the purpose of God: they had betrayed Joseph, resisted Moses and disobeyed God in the wilderness.

7.44–53. Stephen's defence. It is only in vv. 44–50 that the question of the temple is raised, and if this section represents the position Stephen had been taking, one can understand the indignation of the Jews. The argument here suggests that the building of the temple was in fact contrary to God's will, since it attempted to tie God down to one place.

In vv. 51–3 we see the point of the long preamble: those who now accuse Stephen are following in the footsteps of previous generations; just as they resisted the Holy Spirit, rejecting and killing the prophets, so they have put to death the Righteous One, whose coming the prophets foretold. It is not Stephen who is guilty of disobedience to the Law, but his accusers, since they failed to see that it pointed forward to Jesus.

7.54–60. The martyrdom of Stephen. The fury of the Sanhedrin is understandable But worse was to come. The climax of Stephen's speech is his declaration, in v. 56, that the one whom they had put to death as a blasphemer was now standing at the right hand of God in glory. This is the only occasion when the phrase 'the Son of man' is used outside the gospels as a title for Jesus. The description of Stephen's vision of the Son of man echoes Dan. *7.13* and the declaration of Jesus at his trial as it is given in Lk. *22.69*. If the Son of man is standing rather than sitting, this is perhaps because he is understood to be acting as Stephen's advocate in heaven, acknowledging him as his follower before the throne of God (cf. Lk. *12*.8). Stephen is the first to have acknowledged Christ to the point of death. It is appropriate that he dies with the prayer of Jesus on his lips (v. 60; cf. Lk. *23.34*). The stoning of Stephen for blasphemy is in accordance with the Law (cf. Deut. *15*.5 f.)

but may have been contrary to what Rome permitted (cf. Jn. *19*.31): the scene described by Luke suggests a lynching rather than an official execution.

8.1–4. *Persecution*. It seems strange that the apostles should be spared from a 'great persecution' that scattered 'all' the members of the Church (v. 1). Probably what Luke describes was an attack on the 'Hellenists' in the Church, whose views may have been similiar to those of Stephen: if so, the 'Hebrews' (who probably still continued to worship in the temple) may have been spared for the moment. Instead of destroying the Church, the persecution caused the gospel to spread, since those who fled from Jerusalem preached the word throughout Judea and Samaria, so fulfilling Jesus' command to the disciples in *1*.8.

8.5–8, 14–17. *Samaria*. Philip, one of the seven, now preaches in Samaria—an important step, since Samaritans were of mixed race, and despised by Jews as no better than heathens. But Philip's preaching produces the same results as that of the apostles in Jerusalem. No doubt this is why the apostles send Peter and John to investigate. The idea that the converts in Samaria were baptized, but had to wait for a visit from the apostles to receive the Spirit, has been interpreted by some as an example of the rite of confirmation. Others have used it to support the idea of a 'second baptism' with the Holy Spirit. However, it is clear from other passages that the gift of the Spirit normally accompanied baptism, and that what happened in the case of the Samaritans was unusual. The apostles came to Samaria, not to 'confirm' Philip's converts, but to ratify his extraordinary step in preaching to Samaritans and baptizing them. The gift of the Spirit is a divine confirmation that their conversion is the work of God.

The story of Simon the magician (vv. 9–13, 18–24) demonstrates the misunderstanding of the power of the Spirit which is possible when it is seen in magical terms.

8.26–40. *The Ethiopian eunuch*. Another advance in mission is made, this time as the result of clear divine guidance (v. 26).

The man whom Philip was sent to meet was an Ethiopian, not a Jew; more important, since he was a eunuch, he could not become a proselyte (cf. Deut. 23.1). Since he had been to Jerusalem to worship there, he was presumably a 'God-fearer', a Gentile adherent to Judaism. The passage quoted comes from Isa. 53, which we know today as one of the 'Servant Songs', though in the first century these 'Songs' were not distinguished from the rest of the text. The passage probably referred, originally, to the sufferings of Israel, or the Remnant of Israel, but it was obviously an appropriate text to apply to the sufferings of Christ. Strangely, this passage is not widely quoted in the New Testament, though it played a significant part in later interpretations of Christ's death. One very interesting feature here is that Luke makes no use of the theme of vicarious atonement for sin which is found in the later verses of Isa. 53: he stops his quotation short immediately *before* the words 'he was stricken for the transgression of my people'. For Luke, Isa 53 was important, not because it offered an interpretation of Christ's death as an atonement for sin, but because it supported his belief that the death of Christ was 'necessary', part of God's purpose set out in scripture. It was later theologians who moved on to see in this passage an explanation of the significance of Christ's sufferings.

The eunuch's question in v. 36, together with the reply of Philip and the eunuch's response in v. 37, may indicate the kind of ritual used at early baptisms, when the candidate confessed his faith in Jesus in a simple form of creed. Verse 37 is in fact missing from many mss., and is almost certainly a later addition to the text. We see here an interesting example of the way in which traditions were used by the Christian community and adapted to provide material relevant to their own situations.

9.1–19. *Paul's conversion.* Paul has already appeared in the story as a witness to Stephen's death and a persecutor of the Church (8.1, 3). Throughout these early chapters he is referred to as 'Saul'; Luke switches names at 13.9, at the point where Paul arrives in Cyprus. The move to Gentile territory is an appropriate place to make this change, since 'Saul' was a Jewish name, 'Paul' one of the three names which Paul would have used as a Roman citizen. Paul's conversion is described three times in Acts, and the details vary (cf. 22.1–21; 26.4–23). Christians are described here as those belonging to 'the Way'. Paul himself describes his conversion experience in terms of 'seeing the Lord' (1 Cor. 9.1; 15.8). Luke thinks in terms of glory, symbolized by the light (v. 3). The bond between Jesus and his followers is such that Paul is accused of persecuting Jesus in his persecution of the Church.

There is no evidence for the popular belief that Paul's conversion marked the end of a long interior struggle. According to Luke's account here, his conversion was sudden, dramatic and totally unexpected. This is supported by Paul's own description of his 'monstrous' or 'untimely' birth (1 Cor. 15.8). The word he uses actually means 'abortion', and Paul is perhaps trying to describe the abruptness of his conversion.

Paul's conversion was tied up with his call to be an apostle to the Gentiles. He himself spells this out in Gal. 1.16. Here, we learn it in the words of the Lord to Ananias (v. 15; cf. 22.14 f. and 26.16 f.).

9.20–31. *Paul preaches the gospel.* Luke describes the amazement of Jews and Christians alike at Paul's conversion. Like the twelve before him, he now preaches 'boldly in the name of the Lord' (v. 29). Luke says nothing about a visit to Arabia (cf. Gal. 1.17); perhaps because he did not know of it, perhaps because it was not relevant to his story: according to him, Paul went straight from Damascus to Jerusalem, where the apostles eventually accepted him. Luke seems to have telescoped events, for Paul insists that it was three years before he went back to Jerusalem, and even then he stayed only a short time (Gal. 1.18–20). But he may well have been right in recording that Paul was soon found disputing with 'Hellenists' (here plainly *non*-Christian Greek-speaking Jews)—i.e. the very people who had initiated Stephen's death. Soon his life, too, is in danger, and he has to leave the city for Tarsus (cf. Gal. *1*.21–3). With his departure, the church had peace—which once again suggests that the real friction at this time was between the 'Hellenist' wing of the church and traditional Judaism.

9.32–43. *Peter strengthens the church.* Luke's next few chapters are concerned with Peter and the beginning of the Gentile mission. First, he describes a pastoral visit by Peter to the Christian communities in Lydda and Joppa, in the course of which he heals a paralytic and raises a woman from the dead: the two stories remind us of miracles performed by Jesus (cf. Lk. *5*.17–26; *8*.49–56), and show us how the church is continuing the work of her master.

10.1–48. *The conversion of Cornelius.* This story is of great significance to Luke, and he therefore tells it in detail. From the description given in v. 2, Cornelius seems to have been another 'God-fearer'. His devotion is acknowledged by a heavenly messenger, who commands him to send for Peter (vv. 3–8). Meanwhile Peter also experiences a vision while at prayer and receives a heavenly command (vv. 9–16). There is no doubt in Luke's mind that the step which is about to take place is the result of divine activity. Unlike the explicit directions given to Cornelius, the message given to Peter was obscure (v. 17). The animals which he saw were 'common' or 'unclean', i.e. those which Jews were forbidden to eat, and the command to kill and eat them shocked him. But he is assured that the divine command to eat them has made them clean. The threefold repetition of the scene underlines its importance.

The meaning of the vision becomes clear in subsequent events. Prompted by the Spirit, Peter goes to visit Cornelius in his home, though it was contrary to the Mosaic Law for Jews to mix with Gentiles in this way. He recognizes, however, that through the vision, God has commanded him 'to call no man common or unclean' (v. 28): the distinction between Jew and Gentile has been removed. The question of the admission of Gentiles to the church was a complex one because it was linked with the question of Jewish food laws. Jewish

123

Christians who ate with Gentile Christians inevitably broke the Mosaic food laws. Since Christian worship was based on a common meal, the Gentile mission raised the whole problem of 'table fellowship' between Jews and Gentiles and the question of the continuing validity of the Mosaic Law. The story of Cornelius reflects the conviction which came to be shared by more and more Christians that they must not treat Gentiles as 'common' or 'unclean'. That in turn suggested that it was permissible to eat food which had previously been shunned as unclean by the Jews.

The story of Cornelius' vision (vv. 30–3) is repeated, reminding us that this meeting is the result of divine activity. Peter acknowledges that, after all, God shows no partiality towards Jews, and gives a brief summary of the gospel (vv. 34–43). The effect is dramatic: the Holy Spirit comes on all his hearers (Cornelius and his family and friends, v. 24); they too, are heard speaking in tongues, to the amazement of Peter's companions (vv. 44–6). The coming of the Spirit demonstrates that Peter was right to conclude that God shows no partiality towards Jews. The gift of the Spirit was believed, normally, to accompany baptism, but on this occasion it preceded baptism. There could have been no clearer indication that it was right to baptize Cornelius and his friends without further delay. In 8.14–17 the coming of the Spirit gave the divine seal of approval to the baptism of Samaritans; here it compels the baptism of Gentiles. Convinced by what has happened, Peter remains several days in a household which he would previously have thought unclean.

11.1–18. The Jerusalem Church approves. It is not surprising if Peter's action provoked criticism from his fellow Christians. So far they had seen their faith entirely in terms of the fulfilment of God's promises to Israel. Christians had not thought of themselves as belonging to a new religion, but as the faithful group in Israel who had accepted God's Messiah. If Gentiles were now to be admitted to the Christian community, they assumed that it must be by becoming Jews: they must be circumcised and must obey the regulations of the Jewish Law. When Luke refers to 'the circumcision party' in v. 2, he

124

seems to be thinking of the group which emerged in opposition to the Gentile mission—a group of Jewish Christians who continued to insist that Gentile converts must be circumcised. He suggests here that the opposition was silenced (v. 18), but it is clear from later chapters in Acts, as well as from Paul's letters, that the matter was by no means settled at this early stage. What Luke was concerned to stress here was that the apostles and their companions were convinced by Peter's account of what had happened: if they gave their approval to the Gentile mission, then in Luke's view this meant that the later protests on the part of 'the circumcision party' did not represent the position of the Jerusalem authorities.

11.19–26. *The mission to Syrian Antioch.* Luke has already told us, in ch. *8*, that the persecution of the church led to a mission to Samaria; now he describes another result of that persecution—the spread of the gospel to Antioch. Those who brought the gospel do not seems to have been official 'missionaries'. As in Caesarea, so in Antioch, Gentiles ('Greeks', RSV, 'pagans', NEB) respond to the gospel. The Church in Jerusalem is still uneasy about this new development, so they send Barnabas to investigate, who approves what has happened, and takes charge, together with Paul, of the work there. It is perhaps not surprising if the name 'Christian' was first used in Antioch (v. 26), for the church was no longer a wholly Jewish group, and was beginning to be seen as a community distinct from Judaism: the 'Christians' needed a name—though whether they chose it or were given it by others we do not know.

11.27–30. *Christian aid.* The famine gave an opportunity to the Christians in Antioch to demonstrate their solidarity with the 'mother church' in Jerusalem. At a later period, Paul attached great importance to the contributions made to the Jerusalem community by his Gentile churches (cf. 1 Cor. *16*.1–4; 2 Cor. *8–9*), since these gifts were a sign that the Gentiles belonged to the Christian community. The way in which writers select the themes appropriate to their particular purposes is demonstrated by the fact that Luke does not refer to these later gifts (except obliquely, in *24*.17), though he records this so-called famine visit; Paul, on the other hand, does not refer to the aid given on this occasion, even though he is probably describing this visit in Gal. *2*.1–10.

12.1–4. *Martyrdom of James.* The fact that James, one of the twelve, is now put to death, suggests that persecution is no longer directed only against the Hellenists. As in the case of Stephen, there are echoes of the passion narrative: Luke is the only evangelist who says that Herod played a role in the death of Jesus (Lk. *23*.6–12), and now he describes Herod as responsible for the death of James and the imprisonment of Peter; these events take place 'during the days of Unleavened Bread'—i.e. at Passover.

Luke now relates the story of the imprisonment and escape of Peter (vv. 6–19), followed by an account of the death of Herod (vv. 20–3). In spite of everything, the church continues to expand (v. 24).

13.1–3. *The mission from Antioch.* Now comes an important new step. Barnabas and Paul, having returned to Antioch (*12*.25), are commissioned by the church there (now acting independently of the Jerusalem church) to take the gospel elsewhere. This mission takes place at the direct command of the Holy Spirit. Luke apparently regards Barnabas as still the more important figure, since he names him first in v. 2 (cf. *11*.30 and *12*.25). The two men are commissioned by the laying-on of hands, signifying that they are sent as representatives of the Christian community in Antioch.

13.4–*14*.28. *Mission to Asia Minor.* The new venture takes Barnabas and Paul first of all to Cyprus (vv. 4–12). Already we see here features which reappear constantly throughout the rest of Acts: we shall find Paul preaching first in the Jewish synagogues (as in v. 5), even though the great majority of the Jews reject his message while Gentiles welcome it; moreover, the Jews are often responsible for stirring up opposition to Paul, while the Roman authorities are kindly disposed towards him. In this story, Elymas (or Bar-Jesus) typifies the Jewish opposition to the gospel (v. 8), Sergius Paulus the Gentile interest and Roman tolerance (vv. 7, 12).

After preaching in Cyprus, 'Paul and his company' (v. 13: note that Paul has now taken over the role of leader) sail to the mainland. In Antioch (i.e. Antioch in Pisidia, vv. 13–52), the pattern of Jewish rejection and Gentile conversion is repeated. Paul goes first to the synagogue (v. 14), and Luke gives us a summary of his address there—a brief account of Israel's history (vv. 16–22) and the Christian claim that Jesus is the promised descendant of David (vv. 23–32); the final section (vv. 33–41), a scriptural proof of the resurrection and call to repentance, is very similar to Peter's speech in Acts 2.25–39. The claim that anyone who believes in Jesus is 'justified from' (v. 39, RSV 'freed from', NEB 'acquitted of') everything from which one could not be 'justified' by the Law of Moses reminds us of Pauline teaching—even though Paul himself never puts it this way in his letters. Possibly Luke has put into Paul's mouth a typical Christian sermon, and concluded it with what he considers to be a typical Pauline emphasis.

In spite of initial interest on the part of the Jews (vv. 42–4), Jewish opposition was soon aroused (v. 45), with the result that Paul and Barnabas turned their attention to the Gentile population instead, seeing in this the fulfilment of scripture (v. 47). It is interesting to compare this repeated pattern of Jewish failure to respond to the gospel leading to the conversion of Gentiles with Paul's argument in Rom. 9–11.

A similar pattern is seen in Iconium (14.1–7) and Lystra (14.8–20), but Luke tells us little or nothing about the other cities visited. The conclusion of the apostles, when they returned home to the church in Antioch to report, is that 'God has opened a door of faith to the Gentiles' (v. 27).

15.1–35. *The Council of Jerusalem*. This chapter raises very difficult historical problems. The question of Gentile admission to the Church had apparently been settled in *11*.18. Yet here we find Jewish Christians still arguing that Gentile converts to Christianity must accept the same obligations as Gentile converts to Judaism: i.e. they must be circumcised and they must keep the Jewish Law. We know from Paul's letters that this debate went on for a long time, and it is clear that the issue was not settled even by the meeting which Luke describes in this chapter. Luke was perhaps anxious to stress that the apostles were in agreement on this matter; if anyone took a different line, this was contrary to the policy which had been agreed by the Church's leaders. Paul's account of the dispute in Gal. 2.11–19 (if indeed it relates to the same occasion) indicates that Peter (Cephas) was by no means certain about what should be done, and suggests that James belonged to the 'circumcision party'. It is not surprising that the problem took a long time to solve. It must have seemed entirely logical to the majority of Jewish Christians that Gentiles who accepted Jesus as the Jewish Messiah should become Jewish proselytes in the normal way. Once Gentiles were admitted without the requirement that they must submit to circumcision and obey the Jewish Law, it was impossible to contain the Christian community within Judaism: the Christian community began to be seen as a new movement, rather than simply the fulfilment of Jewish hopes. Moreover, it meant that Jewish Christians who recognized Gentiles as fellow Christians could no longer continue to live as Jews, since to eat with Gentiles meant abandoning the food-regulations which had separated the Jews from other nations. The admission of the Gentiles on equal terms was therefore a momentous step, and it was taken with considerable misgivings by many, and not at all by some. There is no doubt that it changed the character of Christianity and the whole course of Church history. Luke, writing at a time when the problem was virtually settled, has no doubt that what happened was the work of the Holy Spirit, and that this was revealed to all the apostles at the time. What seems obvious with hindsight is not necessarily clear to those confronted with the problem, however, and this explains why Paul's account gives a rather different picture.

Nevertheless, it is extremely difficult to harmonize Paul's accounts of his visits to Jerusalem with those recorded by Luke. The most likely view is that the visit referred to in Gal. 1.18–24 corresponds to Acts 9.26–30, and the one described in Gal. 2.1–10 to Acts 11.30 and 12.25. What is strange, however, is that Paul never refers, either here or elsewhere, to the 'Council' of Acts 15, or to the letter sent to the Gentile Christians by the apostles. One wonders whether, in fact, Paul would ever have agreed to such a letter, since it imposed demands upon the Gentile Christians. It seems odd, too, that in Acts 21.25 he apparently hears about this letter for the first time! Once again, the problem may arise out of the different situations of the two authors: perhaps Luke assumes that Paul (the apostle to the Gentiles) must have known about the decision in Jerusalem, and that his Gentile mission was in fact 'authorized' by the Church there. We see from this incident how important it is not to try to force our different pieces of evidence to agree with one another: we do not have enough material to produce a clear 'history' of the developing church, and we should not try to do so. We must be content with a series of 'snapshots'—some of which are badly out of focus.

The people who caused the trouble in Antioch came from Jerusalem (vv. 1, 24), and perhaps claimed that their attitude was in line with the policy of the Church in Jerusalem—where, however, the problems of a 'mixed Christian community' had probably not yet arisen. Those who insisted that it was impossible to become a Christian except by becoming a Jew are said to have been Pharisees; in view of their background, their conviction that Gentiles must accept circumcision and the Law is not surprising. The speech of Peter (vv. 7–11) points back to the conversion of Cornelius, and is backed up by an account of the Gentile mission undertaken by Barnabas and Paul (v. 12) and a quotation from scripture (vv. 13–18). James (v. 13, presumably James the brother of the Lord) takes part in the proceedings as a recognized leader (cf. already 12.17 and Gal. 1.19, 1 Cor. 15.7). His suggestion as to what should be required of Gentile converts is accepted by the gathering (vv. 19–29): they are asked to abstain from meat sacrificed to idols, from 'what is strangled and from blood'—i.e. from meat which had not been drained of blood as the Jewish Law required—and from unchastity. This last requirement is a somewhat odd one to be linked with the rules about food, and there is some manuscript evidence that it is a later addition to the text: if so, then what was set out were the conditions on which Jewish and Gentile Christians might eat together, and these conform with the requirements set out in Lev. *17*.8–14 for 'the house of Israel and the strangers that sojourn among them'. Verses 30–5 describe the reception of the letter in Antioch. Verse 34 is omitted from recent translations because it is missing from most manuscripts: it looks like an attempt to explain how Silas came to be in Antioch in v. 40!

15.36–41. *A second journey planned.* Paul and Barnabas decide to undertake a 'follow-up' to their earlier mission, but in fact they quarrel, and therefore part company. We hear no more of Barnabas, and the rest of Acts is concerned with the travels and preaching of Paul. We shall not study the remaining thirteen chapters of Acts in detail, since it seems better to let Paul speak for himself, and to study his teaching through his letters rather than through the eyes of Luke. Nevertheless, one should certainly read Luke's account of Paul's missionary work, and an outline of these final chapters is provided in the next study.

Read *Groundwork* 29 and 34.

Suggestions for further reading

* G. W. H. Lampe on *Acts* in *Peake's Commentary*.
* F. F. Bruce, *Acts* (New London Commentary, Marshall, Morgan and Scott).

Chapter 7

St. Paul—Apostle to the Gentiles

Passages for special study:

Galatians *1*.1–17; *2*.15–21; *3*.1–4; *4*.11; *5*.1–6, 13–25.
Philippians *1*.27–*2*.15; *3*.1–21.
1 Thessalonians *1*; *4*.1–*5*.11.

MOST of what the New Testament tells us about Paul's life
and work comes to us through the pages of Acts. Our first-
hand knowledge—i.e. what Paul himself tells us—is, of course,
of primary importance, and must always be treated as more
reliable than the information given us by Luke (see *Groundwork* 34c–d). Unfortunately, however, the picture provided
by Paul is only fragmentary, since he does not set out to tell his
readers about himself. Nevertheless, he does at times refer to
his background and life when these are relevant to what he is
writing: that he does so at all is largely due to the fact that Paul
seems to have been under constant attack from opponents
who questioned his authority and his understanding of the
gospel. For this reason, whenever Paul speaks of his calling he
is on the defensive, emphasizing that his gospel and authority
both came from God, and that the success of his mission
demonstrates the power of God, working through his own
weakness. Because we so often read passages from the
Pauline letters out of context, and forget the background
against which they were written, it is easy to gain a false
impression of Paul. Many people think of him as an extremely
self-opinionated little man, who was for ever blowing his own

131

trumpet; this is unfortunate, since the truth seems to have been very different. If we look carefully at Paul's 'boastings', we find that he never boasts of his own achievements and abilities; he boasts only in what he believes God has done in and through him, and he does even this only because others have denied the truth of his gospel, and he is forced to affirm it by pointing to what God has achieved through his preaching.

Galatians

This kind of personal attack lies behind Paul's letter to the *Galatians*. There has been much debate about the date of this letter, and about the precise identity of the Galatians. But the cause of the letter is clear enough. The Galatian Christian community consisted mainly of Gentile converts, who had responded to Paul's preaching of the gospel. Since Paul's departure they have been unsettled by other men (probably Jewish Christians, though they could be Gentiles who had been converted to a Jewish form of Christianity) who had persuaded them that Paul's version of the gospel was deficient, and that in order to be full Christians they must accept not only baptism into Christ, but circumcision and obedience to the Jewish Law as well. Paul, they suggested, was not a true apostle, and his gospel not the full one. It is in response to this situation that Paul sets out his claim to be an apostle through the calling of God himself (*1*.1) and declares that the gospel he has preached to them is the only true one (*1*.6–9). He has not (as has been suggested) preached to them only half of the gospel in order to win favour (*1*.10); the gospel he preached was entrusted to him by God himself when he called Paul to be an apostle (*1*.11–17). Paul gives us here his account of what we know as 'the Damascus Road' experience; he mentions his own former zeal for Judaism and its traditions—not out of any pride, but because these are the very things which his opponents are urging to be an essential part of the gospel: Paul, on the contrary, has abandoned these things for the sake of the gospel! Paul's sense of vocation is seen in v. 15 (cf. Isa. *24*.1, 5; Jer. *1*.5; Luke *1*.15), and in v. 16 we see how closely he connected what we term this conversion with his call to preach to the Gentiles.

In the next verses (16b–22), Paul maintains his independence of the Jerusalem apostles—his gospel was given to him by God, not men. This theme is continued in *2,* though the argument is extremely obscure, because we do not have enough information about the events Paul describes. In vv. 15–21, however, he sets out his understanding of the consequences of the gospel. Man is not 'justified' (i.e. restored to a right relationship with God) by his own attempts to keep the Law, but by the grace of God—not by works of the Law, but through faith in Christ (vv. 15–16). So far Paul and his opponents seem to have been in agreement; but at this point the latter argued that the only way to obey God's will and avoid further sin was to accept the demands of the Jewish Law (v. 17); Paul, on the contrary, maintained that the Law as a way of life had come to an end in Christ. Man on his own could not keep the Law and please God—that was what the gospel was all about (v. 18); the Christian had died to the old life and had found a new way of life in Christ (v. 19). Paul's understanding of what this means is summed up in v. 20: he has died with Christ—Christ now controls him, so that his whole life is a response to God's love. To insist now that men and women can only be righteous in God's sight if they obey the Law is to return to Judaism, and to deny that anything has been achieved in the death and resurrection of Christ.

The logic of Paul's position is driven home in ch. 3. The Galatians are denying the gospel that Paul preached—the gospel of Christ crucified and risen (v. 1). The new life that came to them—the life of the Spirit—came to them because of their faith, not because they had kept the Law (v. 2). Paul here contrasts 'the Spirit' and 'flesh', not because he thinks of man as consisting of 'two parts', but because in Hebrew thought 'the Spirit' represents the eternal power of God, 'flesh' the frailty of man—cf. Isa. *31.*3: for Paul the Law (in spite of its divine origin) belongs to the sphere of 'flesh' and man's frailty.

At this point in the argument Paul introduces the figure of

133

Abraham, probably because his opponents had been maintaining that if the Galatians wished to become true children of Abraham—i.e. to inherit the promises that God had made to him—then they must do so by accepting circumcision and the regulations of the Jewish Law. Paul declares that, on the contrary, since Abraham himself was 'justified' by God on the basis of his faith (v. 6) *before* he was circumcized, and centuries before the Law was given (v. 17), the true children of Abraham are those who share his faith, not his circumcision! (vv. 6–9). Paul now maintains that those who lived under the old covenant lived in fact under a curse (v. 10); nobody was able to keep the Law, or to win God's approval through it, since he had decreed that it was through *faith* that man should be justified (v. 11), and the ways of the Law (where one attempts to justify oneself by works) and of faith (which means reliance upon God) are contrary (v. 12). The curse has, however, been annulled for those who are 'in Christ'. For Paul, this can be demonstrated by reference to scripture: that the curse of the Law rested on Christ himself is seen in Deut. *21.23*—a passage which Paul must have used before his conversion in arguing against the Christian gospel (v. 13); but the resurrection of Christ has meant that the curse has been annulled, and the blessing of God is no longer confined to Jews, but is available to Gentiles (v. 14). Just as death has been transformed into life, so the curse has been transformed into blessing. The promises of God to Abraham have been fulfilled in Christ, who is the true descendant of Abraham (v. 16); the Law was a temporary measure, and it did not alter God's original covenant with Abraham (vv. 15, 17 ff.). Paul uses here the metaphor of the *paidagogos*—'tutor' is an unfortunate translation, since the Greek word refers not to the teacher, but to the slave who was entrusted with the supervision of the young child, and escorted him to school (vv. 23–5); the Law had a similar role as a restraining force, but now is no longer needed, because those who are 'in Christ' have come into their inheritance. Paul has moved, now, from thinking of Christians as 'sons of Abraham' to the idea that they are (in Christ) 'sons of God' (vv. 26–7); but here, the normal laws of inheritance (which excluded non-Jews, women and slaves) do not apply: all are in Christ, and therefore all inherit the promise (vv. 28–9).

In the opening verses of ch. 4, Paul elaborates this idea of Christians as heirs: until Christ came Jews and Gentiles alike were kept under restraint, like children until they come of age (vv. 1–3); but at the appointed time, they changed their status from slaves to sons—not because they had 'come of age', but because they received adoption as sons. This happened because God sent his Son to share their condition of slavery, so that they might share his sonship—and this new status is demonstrated by the fact that Christians possess the Spirit, and call God 'Abba', using the very term which Jesus himself used (vv. 4–7). The old life was in Paul's view one of bondage to hostile forces; and the Galatians now want to return to bondage, by binding themselves to keep the Jewish Law (vv. 8–10). For Paul, slavery (whether to pagan gods or to the Law) and freedom stand opposed (5.1): on the one hand are circumcision and the Law, on the other Christ and the Spirit. For those who have been baptized into Christ to turn now to the Jewish way of salvation, is to confess that faith in Christ is not enough (vv. 2–6). This freedom, however, must not be misinterpreted: some had suggested that Paul's understanding of the gospel meant freedom to sin! On the contrary, says Paul, *freedom* means living by the *Spirit*—a way of life totally opposed to that where man is in *bondage* to the desires of the *flesh* (vv. 16–18); the 'works of the flesh' (NEB 'the kind of behaviour that belongs to the lower nature') and 'the fruit of the Spirit' are spelt out by Paul in vv. 19–24.

Philippians

Another 'autobiographical' passage is found in *Philippians 3*. This letter (written from prison) perhaps dates from the end of Paul's life, but the situation that led him to write this chapter is in some ways similar to that in the Galatian churches; once again, Paul is arguing against those who distort the gospel, and though the Philippian Christians do not seem to have succumbed to this teaching, he nevertheless warns them of its dangers. He speaks here with some bitterness of those who insist on circumcision and so, in his view, place confidence in 'externals' (vv. 1–2; the opening words of the chapter are not necessarily to be translated 'farewell', as in NEB; the RSV rendering, 'finally, my brethren, rejoice in the Lord' is perhaps better). For Paul, the only basis for confidence or pride is Christ (v. 3). The absurdity of priding oneself on those things which are prized by Paul's opponents is demonstrated by his own example, for if anyone could have boasted in the purity of his Jewish descent and his zeal for the Law it was Paul (vv. 4–6). Yet all such ground for boasting and self-justification have been abandoned by Paul: he has treated them all as refuse, for the one thing that matters is to be found in Christ—only there is righteousness to be found (vv. 7–9). He is content to share the abuse and sufferings of Christ, knowing that in doing so he shares also in his life (vv. 10–11). This conformity with Christ is, however, a continuing process, and the final goal lies in the future (vv. 12–14).

This passage referring to Paul's own experience is found in a section in which Paul is urging the Philippians to see that their conduct is 'worthy of the gospel of Christ' (*1*.27). This means that they are to stand firm in the face of opposition and persecution (*1*.27–30) and that they are to do this in one mind, with one spirit. This theme of unity is elaborated in ch. *2*, where Paul appeals to the Philippians to demonstrate in their lives those qualities that in fact belong to the Christian community; each member is to demonstrate love, unselfishness and humility. Verses 6–11 are well known, and it has been suggested that they were also well known to the Philippians—i.e. Paul is here quoting a 'hymn' about Christ; they sum up his redeeming activity—his humility and obedience even to death (vv. 6–8) and his exaltation by God (vv. 9–11). It is very probable that the language of this passage has been chosen to bring out the idea of Christ as the 'second Adam', though this has been obscured in the NEB: the phrase 'the divine nature was his from the first' is better translated, as in the RSV, 'he was in the form of God', and may be an echo of Gn. *1*.26. Certainly Adam is pictured in Gn. *3* as trying 'to snatch at equality with God', and as disobedient to God's command, whereas Christ 'made himself nothing' and

136

'humbled himself'; while Adam was punished by death, and lost his lordship over the created world, Christ voluntarily accepted death, and was raised to lordship over all creation. In Christ's example, therefore, we see man as he was meant to be. It is noteworthy, however, that Paul does not merely appeal to the Philippians to imitate the example of Christ; what he urges them to do, in v. 5, is to possess the mind of Christ, to adopt the attitude which is (or should be) theirs, because of their common life in him. This idea is brought out in the paraphrase of the NEB—'let your bearing towards one another arise out of your life in Christ Jesus' (cf. the RSV's more literal rendering: 'have this mind among yourselves, which you have in Christ Jesus'). The attitude seen in Christ is therefore to be worked out in those who share his life (vv. 12–15).

This theme of correct conduct is taken up again in 3.16. Paul himself can humbly claim to be an example, because he is content to accept suffering and humiliation for the sake of Christ, and to give up all human grounds for boasting: to do otherwise is to be an enemy of the Cross—to deny its significance for one's own life, which should be conformed to its meaning (vv. 17–18). Those whose minds 'are set on earthly things' are dominated by selfish desires (v. 19); but those who accept *Jesus* as Lord know that he will finally rule all things. He who was exalted from humiliation to glory will transform our humble bodies and conform them to his likeness (vv. 20–1). The language of these final verses of ch. 3 echoes that of the 'hymn' in ch. 2, and suggests that Paul has in mind here an idea which he elaborates elsewhere: because of Christ's self-emptying and oneness with man, God exalts both him and those who are linked to him in baptism. So those who share his death and resurrection are transformed, as he is, and share his glory: for the Christian, however, this is a gradual process, completed only at death or at the final coming of Christ.

1 Thessalonians

The earliest of all Paul's letters is perhaps 1 *Thessalonians*.

Written after Paul has been forced to leave Thessalonica, it expresses his relief and joy at the news which has reached him of the Christian community's progress, and reminds them gently of the things he taught them by word and example. The letter opens with a salutation; all letters of the period began like this. Some of Paul's letters have more elaborate salutations; here, he links himself with his fellow missionaries, Silvanus and Timothy. Letters usually continued with an expression of thanks—often to the gods. So in *1*.2–10 Paul thanks God for the faithfulness of the Thessalonian Christians; they received the gospel with joy, becoming imitators of the apostles, and now, in turn, they have become an example to others. Paul reminds them, in particular, of two aspects of their conversion which he wishes to underline: they turned from idols to serve a living and true God, and they wait for the appearance of Jesus from heaven (*1*.9 f.).

What 'service of a living and true God' means is elaborated by Paul in ch. *4,* when he tactfully urges his converts to continue trying to please God—only more so! (vv. 1–2). 'Pleasing God' means holiness (vv. 2–3): they must avoid immorality, 'not giving way to lust like the pagans who are ignorant of God' (vv. 3–5); to appreciate the force of what Paul is saying it must be remembered that 'pagan' is precisely what these people had been, only a few months before! In view of the background of these early Christian communities, it is not surprising that Paul had to stress this aspect of Christian living. 'Love of the brethren' is emphasized in vv. 9–12, again with Paul urging his converts to greater efforts.

The other theme is taken up in *4.*13–18. The Thessalonian Christians have apparently been distressed by the death of some of their number, supposing that this meant they would not share in the kingdom of Christ when he returned to earth. Paul assures them that there is no need to grieve: their brothers are 'in Christ' (v. 16—paraphrased in the NEB as 'the Christian dead'), and since Jesus died and rose again, they too will live (v. 14); it will make no difference whether one is alive or dead at the Parousia (i.e. the coming of Christ). Paul, of course, expected Christ to return in the near future, and his description of what would happen follows Jewish

138

ideas about the coming of God in judgement at the final Day
(vv. 16–17). His main concern, however, is that no matter
when this may happen, the Christian shares the life of Christ,
and therefore need not fear. This, of course, is no excuse for
the Christian to be slack, since the Day will come unexpect-
edly—like a thief in the night! Christians must live in accordance with their calling, remembering at all times the day
when God will finally vindicate those who belong to Christ.
1 Thess. 5.10 sums up Paul's understanding of the meaning of
salvation: Christ died for us, in order that we might live—with
him.

You will find brief notes on Galatians, Philippians and
Thessalonians, together with outlines of their contents, in
Groundwork 37h–i, j, m–n, q–s.

If you have time after studying this week's passages, read
through Acts *16–28*. Here is a brief outline of these chapters,
which are concerned entirely with the story of Paul:

16.1–5	Paul revisits Derbe and Lystra
6–40	Paul at Philippi
17.1–9	Thessalonica
10–15	Beroea
16–34	Athens
18.1–17	Corinth
18–23	Paul returns to Antioch, and sets out once more
24–8	Apollos in Ephesus
19.1–41	Paul in Ephesus
20.1–21.14	Paul sets out for Jerusalem
21.15–23.30	Paul in Jerusalem: his arrest
23.31–26.32	Paul in captivity at Caesarea: his defence before Agrippa
27.1–28.14	The voyage to Rome
28.15–31	Paul in Rome

Read *Groundwork* 34c–d.

Suggestions for further reading

* G. Bornkamm, *Paul* (Hodder and Stoughton).

W. Barclay, *The Mind of St. Paul* (Fontana).

Morna D. Hooker, *Pauline Pieces* (Epworth).

L. Grollenberg, *Paul* (SCM).

H. Richards, *St. Paul and His Epistles* (Darton Longman and Todd).

K. Grayston, *The Epistles to the Galatians and the Philippians* (Epworth Preacher's Commentary).

K. Grayston, *Philippians and Thessalonians* (Cambridge NEB Commentary).

Chapter 8

St. Paul—Pastor of the Churches

This study is concerned with Paul's relations with one of his churches, that in Corinth, and is based on the following passages:

1 Corinthians *1*.1–*2*.5; *3*.1–17; *11*.17–26; *12*; *13*;
   14.1–19, 26–33; *15*.1–28, 35–57.
2 Corinthians *1*.1–7; *4*.5–12, 16–18; *5*; *6*.1–10.

THERE can be no doubt that Paul was the first great theologian of the Christian church. Yet he wrote no 'systematic theology' of the kind produced by later theologians. What he did write was a series of letters, addressed to particular situations, and intended to deal with particular problems and difficulties which had risen within the early Christian communities. The result is that what we have in these letters is 'applied' rather than 'pure' theology—the application of the Christian faith to particular problems of belief and conduct. This means, however, that it is extremely difficult for us to grasp the 'whole' Paul, since the record of his teaching is incomplete. Since he was writing to Christians, he did not need to explain to his readers the fundamental features of their faith; normally, he can assume these basic beliefs, and he mentions them only in order to show the reason for what he is now saying, or if he needs to correct some misunderstanding. Paul's theology is therefore somewhat like an iceberg: much of its lies beneath the surface and is invisible to the casual observer.

141

Another problem in trying to reconstruct Paul's thought is in knowing which of the Pauline letters are 'authentic'. Although to the modern mind it seems strange that Christian writers should have attributed their own writings to someone else, this was by no means an unusual custom at the time; those who had succeeded Paul, and had been taught by him, might well feel that what they were writing was Paul's message for their own day, and so—in all humility—attribute their work to him. If we decide that some of the letters are not by Paul himself this is no loss—indeed, it is perhaps gain to discover that there were others in the early Church besides Paul who understood and interpreted the Christian gospel in this way; but it does mean that one must be cautious in using such letters in trying to reconstruct the theology of Paul himself. At one time or another the authorship of most of the letters has been questioned, but Romans, 1 and 2 Corinthians, Galatians and Philemon are usually accepted as the bedrock of Pauline material; most scholars accept 1 Thessalonians and Philippians; there is more doubt about Colossians, and considerable hesitation about 2 Thessalonians and Ephesians; the majority of scholars believe that the Pastorals (1 and 2 Timothy and Titus) are *not* by Paul, though they might include fragments of Pauline letters. The methods used in this attempt to determine the authorship of a letter include the examination of theological ideas (though this can be a somewhat circular argument, since we only know Paul's ideas from his letters) and the scrutiny of particular words—both theologically significant words which Paul uses (or does not use) in other letters, and apparently insignificant words such as the Greek word *kai* (meaning 'and'), since authors tend to use such common words in a constant pattern; a computer has been used to assist in counting, but statisticians and literary experts, as well as New Testament scholars, are still not agreed regarding the conclusions that can be drawn.

Yet another difficulty in trying to understand Paul arises from the very practical purpose of his letters; so much of what he wrote is bound up with aspects of life and ways of thoughts that now seem obscure and irrelevant. The debate as to whether Gentile Christians should be obliged to keep the regulations of the Jewish Law, and whether it was proper to eat the meat offered for sale in the market-place at Corinth from the carcases of animals which had been sacrificed to pagan deities, no longer excites us. Yet it would be wrong to conclude that Paul's teaching on these matters is therefore out of date; for what Paul does in discussing any problem regarding conduct is to go back to first principles and apply his understanding of the gospel to the matter in hand. Although the problems may have changed, Paul's understanding of the relation of the Christian gospel to ethical problems is as relevant to the twentieth century as to the first. If we try simply to apply what he said about one situation to other, totally different problems, then, of course, his teaching is being taken out of context and seems irrelevant; if we try to understand why and how he applied his theological insight to various problems, however, then we may find this helpful in trying to do the same today.

Although Paul is writing to Christians, and does not need to give them a basic account of the gospel, he does frequently remind them of what he regards as central—precisely because, again and again, he argues out the practical consequences of those facts in many spheres. We have already looked at one such statement in 1 Cor. *15*.1–8, and noted how Paul's account of the gospel here can be summed up in four verbs—Christ died, he was buried, he was raised, he was seen. Indeed, we can reduce these to two, for the phrase 'he was buried' serves to confirm the reality of the death, just as the words 'he was seen' confirm the reality of the resurrection. He died; he was raised; this, for Paul, is the basis of the gospel. Of course, in 1 Cor. *15* Paul is concerned in particular with the question of resurrection, so that may have influenced the way he has expressed his basic faith. Let us try another passage—this time Rom. *10*.9, where Paul tells us what Christian confession (i.e. that Jesus is Lord) means: it is to believe that God raised Jesus from the dead. Or again, in the passage in Phil. *2* which we have already studied, we found the same pattern, although there the idea of exaltation, rather than resurrection, was used; but the result was the confession of Jesus as Lord. Wherever we take 'soundings' in the Pauline

143

letters, we find the same basic understanding of the gospel: Jesus died, and was raised by God. Nor is there any reason to disbelieve Paul when he tells us (in 1 Cor. *15*) that this was the tradition which he received.

It is this 'simple' gospel which lies behind the theological obscurity of the Pauline letters. But of course it is not as simple as it appears. For Paul, a Jew, to preach a crucified Christ—or Messiah—was no simple matter. In 1 Cor. *1*.23 he describes the idea of a crucified Messiah as 'a stumbling-block to the Jews'. It was undoubtedly a stumbling-block that had sent Paul himself sprawling. The conviction that came to him that Jesus was the Messiah, and that the Messiah of God had therefore been crucified, meant that he had to re-think all his ideas about God and his own relationship with God. What sort of God was it who acted in this way—who permitted the Messiah's death? That he had indeed acted in this way was proved for Paul beyond all doubt by the resurrection. Paul, who had previously thought that his relationship with God was a matter of his own scrupulous obedience to the Law, found that he had to make room in his thought and life for a crucified Messiah whom God had raised from the dead. But this teaching was not only a stumbling-block to Jews; it was dismissed as utter foolishness by non-Jews, too. Men naturally associate God with glory and power: what, then, was this talk of the Son of God dying in shame and weakness? The simple message of Christ crucified and risen had far-reaching implications.

Some of those implications are worked out for us by Paul in 1 and 2 Corinthians. These two letters represent only part of Paul's correspondence with the Corinthian church, and it is by no means easy to reconstruct the situation behind them; what we do know, however, is that relationships between Paul and the Christian community in Corinth went sadly wrong, and that the trouble seems to have begun because there were those there who challenged Paul's authority and his understanding of the gospel; in many ways, therefore, the situation is similar to that behind Galatians, although the understanding of the gospel that was being put forward seems to have been a Greek one, rather than a Jewish version.

1 Corinthians

In *1 Corinthians* we see the first signs of trouble between Paul and the Corinthian church. There seem to have been two main reasons why Paul wrote this letter. One is that the church has written to him (*7.*1) asking for advice in various matters—probably those with which Paul deals in chs. *7–15*. The other is that disquieting news has come to Paul about the attitudes prevalent in the church, and it is with this—to Paul more urgent—matter that he deals in chs. *1–6*.

The letter opens with the usual salutation (*1*.1–3) and thanksgiving (*1*.4–9). Typically, Paul uses words here that point forward to the themes he is going to take up in the letter, and so reminds his readers of certain ideas which he thinks they are perhaps overlooking. This is somewhat obscured in the NEB, but can be seen more clearly in the RSV: e.g. in v. 2 he writes to those whom God has set apart as his own, his holy people; although the NEB correctly translates this by 'dedicated to him' and 'claimed by him as his own', the Greek implies certain consequences which are brought out by the RSV translation: 'to those sanctified in Christ Jesus, called to be saints'; in view of the Corinthian situation, it was well to remind the Corinthians that they were 'sanctified'! 'Saints' (RSV) or 'those dedicated to God' (NEB) is the common New Testament term for Christians—and before that, of those Israelites who were faithful to God. The tact of Paul is seen in vv. 4–9, where he makes the subject of his thanksgiving the very gifts of which the Corinthians appear to have been boasting, so reminding them that these are the gifts of God.

In *1*.10–17 Paul turns immediately to the news brought to him by 'Chloe's people' (presumably her servants, travelling on business) that there were disputes and divisions within the Corinthian Christian community. It is not clear whether the different groups mentioned in v. 12 held different beliefs about the gospel, or whether what was appearing in the community was some kind of personality cult. Since Paul does not deal specifically with false teaching in these early chapters of Corinthians, it seems probable that it was the latter. The situation is thus not a break-up into denominations, but an emphasis on the role of church-leaders; possibly groups of Christians were 'supporters' of the apostle through whom they had been converted. It is more than likely that we see here the influence of the background of the Corinthians themselves, for they lived in a city where philosophers taught and attracted a circle of followers; naturally the Corinthian Christians tended to think of the apostles in the same way. It is a puzzle to know who the people claiming to belong to Christ were, as one would expect Paul to commend them, rather than link them with the other 'parties'; since they are included in the general rebuke, it seems likely that they were claiming to be in some way superior to the other Christians. Paul, reacting in horror to this situation, gives us in v. 13 one of his terse summaries of the meaning of being a Christian: it was, of course, Christ who was crucified for you, not Paul (or Apollos or Cephas), and it was into the name of Christ (i.e. into his possession) that you were baptized. The identity of the person who performs the rite of baptism is unimportant—so unimportant that Paul cannot precisely remember whom he himself baptized. Here Paul turns from baptism to the character of the gospel, since it is clear from their false emphasis upon the apostles that the Corinthians have misunderstood its implications.

In vv. 18–31 Paul expounds the meaning of the Cross in terms of folly and wisdom. In writing to the Galatians, Paul had been dealing with men who were thinking in Jewish terms; who saw God's revelation in terms of powerful acts, and who believed that it was through obedience to the commands of God that one could win salvation. In writing to the Corinthians, Paul is dealing with men who thought in Greek terms; they saw God's revelation in terms of *gnosis* (knowledge) or *sophia* (wisdom), and believed that it was through this knowledge or wisdom that one won salvation. The difference is summed up by Paul in v. 22. To both Jews and Greeks Paul preaches the gospel of Christ crucified—and to both groups such a message is offensive. To the Jew, the message of a crucified Messiah (the Greek word Christ, 'anointed', would, of course, mean 'Messiah' to all Jews) was a contradic-

146

tion of his understanding of God and his promises; to the Greek, it was sheer foolishness. And in their different ways, both the Galatian and the Corinthian Christian communities were falling back into these positions, because they were refusing to place the Cross at the centre of their lives; the Galatians were trying to justify themselves by the Law, the Corinthians by wisdom. Although their backgrounds and language were so different, their mistake, to Paul, was fundamentally the same: both were trying to 'add' to his gospel—and so undermine it; both were trying to win salvation in their own way and by their own efforts, instead of relying solely on the saving activity and mercy of God. 'This doctrine of the cross' turns human values upside down. Death is transformed into life, weakness is seen to be strength, and folly is found to be wisdom. Those who are 'in Christ Jesus' and one with him, share what he is and has, v. 30, and this solely because of what God has done through him; 'there is no place for human pride in the presence of God', v. 29. At the same time , human wisdom and strength are shown up for what they are—foolishness and weakness. This principle is demonstrated in the case of the Corinthians themselves, who are not much in the eyes of the world, but have been chosen by God, vv. 27–8.

The same principle is also demonstrated in the case of Paul himself (2.1–5). He preached to the Corinthians nothing but the 'simple' gospel of Christ crucified; he did not use rhetoric or offer them 'wisdom'; nor did he come in power, but in weakness. Yet through his proclamation of the gospel God was able to convert the Corinthians; the very fact that they are now Christians at all is the proof of what Paul is saying.

Behind these words of Paul we may perhaps once again detect criticisms that have been levelled at Paul: possibly it had been suggested that, unlike Apollos, he was a poor debater, untrained in rhetoric and philosophy, who did not really understand the full implications of the Christian gospel (2.1–5). If so, then Paul, by admitting his own inadequacies, neatly reverses the argument by demonstrating how God used his weakness and lack of wordly wisdom. It may be that in public debate the trained philosophers of Corinth were able to put rings round Paul and make his 'simple' message of the gospel look foolish; but in his letters Paul certainly shows ability in skilful argument (cf. 2 Cor. *10*.10). The theme of wisdom and folly is continued in the rest of ch. *2*.

3. 1–4 picks up a claim being made by the Corinthians to be 'spiritual' men, who have come to maturity; Paul rejects this claim, declaring that their behaviour demonstrates that they are still infants. The contrast between 'the merely natural plane' (lit. 'belonging to the sphere of flesh') and 'people who have the Spirit' (lit. 'belonging to the sphere of the Spirit') is precisely that which we met in Galatians *5*.13–25. The truth of what Paul is saying is seen in their divisions, which demonstrate how human—not spiritual—their behaviour is.

The correct way to look at the apostles is spelt out in the next section. Paul and Apollos are simply servants (*diakonoi*) through whom the Corinthians came to Christian faith (*3*.5). They are like gardeners, planting and watering seed—all of no use unless God makes the seed grow (*3*.6–9). They are like builders—and the building they are working on is the Christian community. The foundation is Christ himself, and the building is the temple of God, because the Spirit of God dwells there (*3*.10–17). Those who lead the Church are all like workers on a building site—but they must be careful what materials they add to the building, since their work will one day be tested by fire. Paul's metaphor has become somewhat confused here—wood might be a more suitable building material than gold!—but the choice is governed by the idea of testing with fire.

In the rest of ch. *3* and ch. *4*, Paul continues the same theme. In ch. *5* he turns to another disturbing piece of news which has reached him—a case of grave sexual immorality. Paul is shocked, not simply by the occurrence of immorality, but by the complacency of the Christian community about it. To understand the Corinthian attitude, one has to remember that what we term immorality was common in the pagan world, and that Corinth was itself famed for the prostitutes attached to the temple of Aphrodite; converts to Christianity from paganism did not naturally associate religion and morality. Paul deals with this kind of problem in chs. 5 and 6.

In ch. 7, Paul deals with a totally different attitude—one that advocates celibacy; Paul, although agreeing that celibacy is a gift given by God to some (7.1, 7, 8), argues that for most it is right to marry. By stressing the verses where Paul agrees with his correspondents, and ignoring the rest of the chapter, commentators have sometimes given a completely contrary picture of Paul. In vv. 25–35, certainly, Paul explains that in his view it is better not to marry, though he stresses that this is only his opinion; it is important to realize the reason for this opinion—his belief that the Parousia is near, and that before then there will be a time of great trouble, when family ties could add to sorrow.

Chapters 8–10 are concerned with one problem—that of 'food consecrated to heathen deities', and whether a Christian should eat it. Paul's chief argument is that those who claim to 'have knowledge' and who believe that there is no harm in the meat, since the so-called 'deities' do not exist, must beware of upsetting their weaker brothers; if they persuade them to do something that their conscience tells them is wrong, they are leading them into sin, and so destroying them—the brothers for whom Christ died. So, concludes Paul, 'if food be the downfall of my brother, I will never eat meat any more' (8.13). In ch. 9 Paul gives an example of this willingness to give up something for the sake of Christ—in this case, his own right to support, as an apostle, from the Christian community. The argument is somewhat involved, since Paul has to prove his right to be maintained, in order then to demonstrate that he has foregone this right! Behind the chapter, one detects again possible accusations that Paul is not a 'proper' apostle—this time on the ground that he did not receive support from the Church. In ch. 10 Paul returns to the theme of 'tainted' meat—this time with a warning to the 'knowledgeable' not to be too confident.

Chapter 11 is concerned with two matters regarding worship. The first, the 'covering' of women's heads, is dealt with in vv. 1–16. So much attention has been paid to the fact that Paul thought it proper for a woman to have her head covered

149

during worship, that the fact that he assumed that women would be taking part in praying and prophesying (an amazing assumption in view of the contemporary Jewish customs in worship) has been almost overlooked. Verses 17–34 are more important to us, since they give us the earliest account of the institution of the Lord's Supper. That we have this account at all is due only to the misconduct of the Corinthian Christian community. It seems difficult to believe that the Corinthians themselves consciously linked the death of Jesus with a meal at which they became tipsy, or that they recited the 'words of institution', as later became customary: the emphasis for them was clearly on the joy of their new life. Paul reminds them that in breaking bread together, and drinking the common cup, they are looking back to the death of Jesus, and the covenant made through his blood, by which they became the people of God (vv. 23–5); the meal is also a looking forward, to the time when the Lord will finally come (v. 26); and it is a present fellowship with others, who are also members of Christ—which is why their factions and rude behaviour towards one another are so shocking (vv. 17–22). Once again splits were observable in the Corinthian Church—perhaps the result of social differences in a diverse community.

Chapters *12–14* are concerned with spiritual gifts. The gift that was apparently commonest—and certainly most prized —in the Corinthian Church was that of tongues. So much emphasis was placed upon it that the ability to speak in tongues was apparently being regarded as *the* sign that a man possessed the Holy Spirit. Paul denies that this is so. For him, the fact that a man or woman confesses Jesus as Lord is a sign of the activity of the Spirit (*12*. 1–3). In *12*. 4–11 he lists various activities, all of them gifts of the Spirit, and necessary to the Christian community and he places 'tongues' (NEB 'ecstatic utterance') at the end of his list. The point is driven home in the metaphor of the body in vv. 12–31. Just as the body is a unity, but consists of many different limbs and organs, so it is with those who have been baptized into Christ; they are one in him, and they possess one Spirit, but each has a different function. Just as there would be chaos in a body if every member had the same function, so it is with the body of Christ in the Christian community; God gives different gifts to different members of the body, and each has his or her role to play—and once again (v. 30) ecstatic utterance and its interpretation come last in Paul's list.

It was natural that the Corinthians would prize the gift of tongues—a showy gift, which indicated to the community that the spirit was mightily at work. Paul, however, refuses to acknowledge it as a superior gift. For him, the highest gifts are those that build up the Christian community, and the best of all is love (v. 13). The word translated 'love', *agape*, is a biblical, not a classical one, and means primarily God's love for us; the more common Greek terms were *eros,* physical desire, and *philia,* friendship. It is notable that the characteristics of love listed here by Paul seem to be precisely those qualitites lacking in the Corinthian church, whose members boasted in their ability to speak in tongues and to prophesy, to know hidden truth and to have faith (vv. 1–3); who were impatient with others, boastful, conceited, and rude (vv. 4–5). Prophecy, tongues and knowledge, so much valued by the Corinthians, are only temporary, but love will last (vv. 8–13).

In ch. *14* Paul takes up again the argument about the value of the gift of tongues, this time arguing that prophecy is a more useful gift, since it serves to build up the church (vv. 1–6). The same test is applied in vv. 26–33; these verses suggest that Christian worship at this stage was entirely 'unstructured' (cf. also *11.*17 ff.). The result appears to have been somewhat chaotic!

The background to ch. *15* appears to be the denial by some of the Christians in Corinth of a future resurrection; what precisely these people did believe, however, it is very difficult to discover. Paul argues from first principles—namely the gospel that he preached to the Corinthians, and that they accepted (vv. 1–2). The summary in vv. 3–5 may be part of an early Christian 'creed', and Paul adds a list of witnesses to the resurrection, of whom he was the last. The gospel is common ground to all, whoever preached it (v. 11).

For Christians to deny the possibility of resurrection is to deny that Christ has been raised from the dead, which is clearly nonsense, since his resurrection is the basis of their faith (vv. 12–19). Christ has been raised from the dead—'the first fruits of the harvest of the dead'. Jesus was raised to life on the day when the first fruits of the barley harvest were offered in the temple; but as the 'first fruits' his resurrection is, as it were , a guarantee of ours. As Adam brought death to all men, so Christ has brought life (vv. 20–2); but the time of the completion of the 'harvest' is the End. Then Christ will return, death will be finally defeated, the dead will be raised, and Christ will hand over his authority to God, who will be all in all (vv. 23–8).

In v. 35 Paul raises two questions: 'How are the dead raised?' and 'In what kind of body?' Verses 36–44 deal with the second question: the resurrection body will not be a physical one, but spiritual. We are to be completely transformed, and the transformation will be as great as that which occurs when an apparently dead seed is thrown into the ground; our humilitation is to be changed into glory (cf. Phil. 3.21), and our weakness into power (cf. 1 Cor. 1.24). The first question is taken up in vv. 45 ff., which explain how this happens. Just as the first man, Adam, was made by God 'an animate being'—i.e. living within this earthly sphere—so Christ, who is the 'last' Adam, has been made by God a life-giving spirit. All mankind shares Adam's nature (his name means 'man'), for like him they are made of the earth, and belong to the earthly sphere; but in the same way we can now share the nature of the heavenly man, Christ. Verses 51–7 explain the change that will be needed; those who are dead when the end comes will be changed, for what is perishable must be clothed with what is imperishable; those who are alive will also be changed, for what is mortal must be clothed with what is immortal. So death will finally be conquered.

The final chapter of 1 Corinthians gives instructions about the collection which Paul is making among his churches, as a gift to the Christians in Jerusalem, and outlines his future plans.

2 Corinthians

Between the writing of 1 and 2 Corinthians, relations be-

tween Paul and the Corinthian community appear to have
deteriorated sadly, and it seems that there was something like
open rebellion to Paul in the Church. Paul paid a very
unpleasant visit to the city (cf. 2 Cor. *12*.14 and *13*.1–2) and
also wrote a stern letter which caused him much anguish (cf.
2 Cor. *2*.1–4, 7.8–9); it is possible that part of this letter is
preserved in 2 Cor. *10–13,* since the tone of these chapters is
harsher than the earlier ones, but it is impossible to be certain
of this. The earlier part of *2* Corinthians, at least, was written
to express Paul's joy at the news brought to him by Titus that
the Corinthians are now ready to accept Paul's guidance.

The opening thanksgiving (2 Corinthians *1*.3–7), which
follows the salutation (vv. 1–2), is a moving statement of
Paul's joy in the comfort that has come to him. Remembering
how in 1 Corinthians he spoke of strength which comes
through weakness, and wisdom through folly, we are not
surprised to find him applying the 'principle of the Cross'
here, and speaking of comfort which comes through suffering.
As Christ's suffering brought consolation to others, so the
apostle, sharing in Christ's suffering, is able not only to share
his consolation, but to be the means of bringing that consolation to others.

Chapters *1* and *2* are concerned with events which have
happened to Paul and to the Corinthians, and with clearing up
any misunderstanding between them.

Chapter *3* takes up the theme of the character of Paul's own
ministry. Paul does not need (as some do) letters of introduction guaranteeing that he is a true apostle; the Corinthian
Christians themselves are proof of his apostleship (vv. 1–3).
In the following verses. Paul compares his own ministry, with
that of Moses—a remarkably bold comparison for a Jew! The
argument is based upon Paul's interpretation of the story of
Moses on Mount Sinai, and reflects his rabbinic training.

In ch. *4*, Paul explains what it means to be a minister of the
new covenant. The apostles do not preach themselves, but
Christ Jesus as Lord (vv. 5–6). We remember from the first
letter that the Corinthians had a tendency to exalt the
apostles, and this is apparently still the case, since in vv. 4 ff.,
Paul does his best to correct such a tendency by describing

153

what the real lot of an apostle is. The glory about which he has been speaking (3.18, 4.6) is not a glory that the world would recognize, for the apostles are hard-pressed, bewildered hunted, struck down. But once again, we see the principle of the Cross at work: it is 'the death that Jesus died' which they carry in their bodies (v. 10)—in order that his life may also be revealed; it is the transcendent power of God (the same power as that which raised Jesus from the dead) which is at work through them (v. 7). The death of Jesus is the source of life to those who share his resurrected life; so now, the apostles, by sharing in the death of Jesus, become the means of bringing his life to their converts (v. 12).

So Paul does not lose heart (vv. 16–18) for he knows that the principle of life through death, glory through decay, is at work in his life—and also in his death (5.1–10). Even if Paul's physical body gives out altogether, he is confident that God will provide another, glorious body for him. Paul shrinks from this, for he does not want to die—though he longs for the future glorious life. There has been much debate on these verses, and discussion as to whether Paul's views here about the future life are different from those expressed in 1 Cor. *15*; it is important to remember that in both passages Paul is using picture language, and that here Paul is not concerned to give teaching about the future life, but rather to express his complete confidence that, whatever may happen to him, God will turn his present humiliations and weakness into glory and strength.

Paul, therefore, as an aspostle, appeals to all men (v. 11). Criticisms have been brought against him, but whatever he has done, and however he has behaved, has not been for personal advantage, but for the sake of the gospel (vv. 12–13). He is compelled by the love of Christ. Verses 14–15 give us another summary of what the gospel means for Paul. What happens in Christ is nothing less than a new creation, and old values have been swept away (vv. 16–17). What happens in Christ is the work of God himself, who has reconciled the world to himself through Christ; and the message of this reconciliation has been entrusted to the apostles, who now act as God's ambassadors (vv. 18–20). In v. 21 we have another terse summary of what happens through Christ—of what 'reconciliation' or 'atonement' means. Christ was made one with man's sinfulness (in his life and his death) so that we, because we are 'in him', might share his righteousness (cf. 1 Cor. *1*.30), and 'be made one with the goodness of God himself'.

Chapter *6* gives further details of the sufferings that the apostles endure and the joy that comes through them—'dying we live' (v. 9). The statement that, though poor, they bring wealth to many (v. 10) finds an echo in *8*.9 in a statement about Christ. This notable verse occurs in a lengthy passage (*8–9*) in which Paul urges the Corinthians to continue faithfully collecting for Christians in Jerusalem; the example of Christ is one reason—and the best—for such generosity.

The later chapters return to the theme of Paul's ministry, but reflect the bitterness of Paul's dispute with the Corinthian Church. To us the most interesting passage is *11*.22–*12*.10, since it tells of Paul's own experiences; for the necessity which drives Paul to 'boast', see the preliminary notes for Study 7.

There are notes about Corinth and the Corinthian letters in *Groundwork* 37d–g.

Suggestion for further reading

M. E. Thrall, *I and II Corinthians* (Cambridge NEB Commentary).

Chapter 9

St. Paul—Theologian

This study centres on the following passages:

Romans *1*.1–6, 16–17; *3*.21–8; *5*; *6*.1–14; *8*; *9*.1–5; *10*.1–4; *11*.1–6, 25–36.

Colossians *1*.13–20; *2*.1–17.

Ephesians *1*.3–14; *2*.11–22; *6*.10–20.

Romans

THE letter to the *Romans* seems to have been written in order to acquaint the church in Rome with Paul's understanding of the gospel and with his missionary policy. While others preach to Israel, Paul feels himself to be called to evangelize the Gentile world, and he explains the part that he believes the Gentiles have in the divine plan: once excluded from the promises by the Law and convenant, they are now called on equal terms with Jews; indeed, the roles seem to have been reversed, for though Israel was once called to be a witness to the Gentile world, it is now the Gentiles who are accepting the gospel, and who will, Paul believes, eventually be the means of bringing Israel to accept God's salvation. Paul is presumably setting out these views because he hopes to begin missionary work in the western world, in Spain (*15*.19–29), and wants the support of the Roman church in this venture: in Romans he comes closer than in any other letter to giving us a full account of his 'theology'.

He begins, in *1*.1–6, by setting out his credentials as an

apostle (vv. 1, 5–6) and by giving a summary of the ⟩
he is commissioned to preach (vv. 3–4): if what we ⟩
is an early form of 'creed', then it is perhaps a state⟩
faith that the Romans would recognize. Once again it in⟩
the idea that Jesus is the Messiah or Christ (born of Da⟩ ⟩s
stock), the statement that he was raised from the dead (raised
by God, rather than 'rose', as in NEB), and that he is Lord. In
the thanksgiving Paul tactfully suggests that the Roman
Christians will be able to encourage him as much as he can
encourage them. In *1.* 16–17 he states the theme of his letter:
the gospel that he preaches 'is the saving power of God for
everyone who has faith; though it came first to Jews, it is
meant also for Greeks (here equivalent to non-Jews, or Gentiles), and it is 'God's way of righting wrong'; it is a gospel
based on and worked out by faith.

The rest of ch. *1* describes the sinfulness and plight of
mankind, and much of its language echoes that used in Gn. *3*
to describe the fall of Adam (or man). When man commits the
basic sin of refusing to obey God and acknowledge him as
God—when he sets up false gods—then he is handed over
('God has given them up', vv. 24, 26, 28) to all manner of sins.
So far the good Jew would have agreed with Paul's analysis,
assuming that he is thinking only of the Gentile world, but in
ch. *2* Paul rounds on the Jew and includes him in the condemnation; those who assert that it is only others who are guilty
are in fact themselves equally guilty, for with all their efforts
to keep the Law they are not truly honouring God but thinking of their own status. So, Paul concludes in *3.* 21–4, no one at
all is without sin; everyone lacks 'the divine splendour' or
glory—a reference to the glory which, according to Jewish
tradition, surrounded Adam, when he spoke face to face with
God and reflected his divine splendour (v. 23). This being so,
'God's way of righting wrong, effective through faith in
Christ', has been revealed. There is no other way of being
'justified'—put into a right relationship with God; the Law is
unable to do it—though, with the prophets, it bears witness
that this is God's way. Paul piles one image on top of another.
What happens to men is an 'act of liberation', a phrase which
translates a Greek word used for the setting free of a slave on

payment of ransom money; men have been set free from the condition of slavery in which they were living (v. 24). Christ's death is described as a 'means of expiating sin', i.e. of removing it (v. 25; the NEB's 'by his sacrifical death' is a paraphrase for 'by his blood'). Paul is using the imagery of an Old Testament sacrifice, in which the blood of the victim was smeared on the altar as a cleansing agent, and symbolized the removal of the sin which separated man from God. The word translated 'means of expiating sin' is also used in the Greek Old Testament to refer to the lid of the ark of the covenant (traditionally translated 'mercy seat'), and so Paul may be thinking in particular of the Day of Atonement, when the high priest sprinkled blood there (cf. Lev. 16.12–17); if so, then he thinks of Christ as at once the victim and the place where reconciliation between God and man is made. Since all depends on God's grace, and not on works of the Law, all human pride is excluded (vv. 27–8).

Romans 4 introduces the objection of a typical Jew to Paul's teaching: What about Abraham? According to the Jewish understanding, Abraham had been justified by his obedience to God's commands; indeed, though he had lived centuries before Moses, he had kept the commandments of the Mosaic code in advance! As in Galatians, Paul reverses the argument: Abraham was accepted by God on account of his faith in God's promises, and not on the basis of works.

Chapter 5 introduces a new section; now that we have been restored to a right relationship with God, what are the consequences? Paul spells out the character of our Christian life: it means *peace* with God, becaue we have been able, through Christ, to enter into this new situation (vv. 1–2); it means *hope* of the divine splendour or glory which now we lack (3.23) but which will one day be restored (the idea that man will finally regain the glory which Adam lost through his sin is part of the Jewish hope for the End, which for Paul is now a *certain* hope); it means *suffering*—but that, like hope, is a ground for joy, since it will be turned to good account (vv. 3–5).

Verses 6–11 set out the basis of our hope: it is the fact that

God has already shown his love for us in the death of Christ. If God loved us to the extent of reconciling us to himself at a time when we were in a state of enmity towards him—and that by the death of his Son—how much more will he save us, now that we are reconciled to him. Note that justification or reconciliation is only a first stage. Salvation—which involves our final sanctification and glorification—lies in the future.

Chapter 5.12–21 is the kernel of the letter, for it sums up Paul's understanding of how salvation comes about 'in Christ'. In the early chapters, Paul has described what man, left to his own devices, is like; his picture is a description of man 'in solidarity with Adam'—man, turning away from God, disobedient and self-willed. In chs. 5–8, however, Paul is telling us about the new life which belongs to those who have been justified by God's gracious act, and his picture is a description of man 'in solidarity with Christ'. Just as his description of the 'old man' was a reflection of the character of Adam, so his description of the 'new man' is a reflection of the character of Christ. All men and women inevitably bear the stamp of Adam, simply by being human; but now there is a new possibility open—that of bearing the stamp of Christ. Adam and Christ are the two patterns for mankind, and of the two, Christ is the greater, since he is man-as-he-is-meant-to-be. In his comparison between them, although Paul uses words like 'as . . . so' (vv. 19, 21), he more often has to explain that what happened in Adam is quite over-balanced by what happened in Christ—as a negative is over-balanced by a positive; so he uses the phrases 'is out of all proportion to' (v. 15), 'is vastly exceeded by' (v. 15), 'is not to be compared with' (v. 16), 'much more' (v. 17). It is easier to follow Paul's argument if vv. 13–14, which are an aside about the Law, are bracketed.

It was through Adam that sin and death entered the world (v. 12); but the gracious gift of God (working through Christ) is much greater than the act of transgression (v. 15); through one came condemnation, through the other acquittal (v. 16); through the wrongdoing of one man, death reigned over mankind, but those who receive God's gift shall reign in life through the one man, Jesus Christ (v. 17). To sum up: the

159

result of one transgression was condemnation for all, the result of one act of righteousness (by Christ) is aquittal and life (v. 18)—i.e. through the disobedience of one man many (='all', a Jewish idiom) were established as sinners, but through the obedience (to death) of one man many will be made righteous (v. 19).

Note that the balance of the sentence in v. 19 seems to imply that Paul expects that all men will eventually be made righteous, i.e. find reconciliation to God and completeness in Christ. If what happens in Christ is 'much more' than what happened in Adam, it must affect all mankind.

Although Paul would have assumed that Adam was an historical person, he has already, in a sense, 'demthyologized' him, by showing that he represents the whole of sinful humanity, and stands for man in his alienation from God.

Chapter 6 returns to the theme of the meaning of this new life in Christ. Some have apparently suggested that if sin leads to grace, one should continue to sin, in order to give further oportunity for grace! (v. 1). Paul rejects this idea as proposterous: Christians have died to sin, and cannot continue in it. How have they died? In the death of Christ. Paul reminds his readers that in baptism they were baptized into Christ, and so became sharers in his death and resurrection life; the reality of this death and resurrection was symbolized in the rite of baptism when they were submerged beneath the water and came up to a new life (vv. 2–4). Paul takes very seriously this idea of union with Christ—indeed, it is the basis of his understanding of how salvation works: because believers die and rise with Christ, they share his condition of being 'right' with God; because his resurrection life flows into their lives, they are being made like him. By sharing in his death, they have died to sin, which dominated their old lives, and are alive to God (vv. 5–11). So they must not allow sin to rule their lives any longer; they are no longer instruments of sin, but of God (vv. 12–14). This theme is elaborated in the rest of ch. 6.

It should be noted that though Paul declares here vigorously that sin belongs to the past life of the Christian, and has no place in his present experience, his letters make it plain that he was well aware that sin could still intrude. In

Rom. 6 he is declaring what *ought* to be, and setting out the logical conclusion of his readers' faith: if they are truly identified with Christ, if they accept fully the meaning of their death to the old life, and resurrection to the new, then sin *cannot* have a hold over them. Unfortunately, however, while they continue to live in this world, they are to that extent still linked to 'Adam', and there is always the possibility that they will slip back into their old existence. So Paul is continually having to remind his readers what their new life involves, and urging them to be what (in Christ) they already are. Contrary to popular opinion, Paul did *not* spend his time thinking and writing about sin. For him, it belonged to the past life, which was dead; Christians should concentrate on the new life, which is found in union with Christ.

Chapter 7 is concerned with the role of the Law, and its inability to deal with sin; since it belongs to the old life, Christians are set free from the Law, too (vv. 1–6). There has been much discussion as to whether vv. 7–25 are autobiographical (Paul uses the first person singular, instead of his more usual 'we'), and if so, whether they refer to Paul before or after his conversion. It must be remembered that Paul is trying to explain why the Law (which was given by God) was unable to bring justification, and so failed to give the life that it promised; the reason is that sin had such a hold on mankind, that it was able to use even the Law to increase its power. We should not read into these verses the idea of an anguished struggle in Paul's mind before his conversion, such as Luther later experienced: rather, he is describing what he now knows to be the case—even the Law, in which he once trusted, had led him further away from God. Although Paul uses the present tense in this passage, he is referring to the 'natural' man who is still in bondage, and not yet 'discharged from the Law' (v. 6).

For those who are in Christ, there is no condemnation (8.1). A new 'law' has appeared—that of the Spirit, which has set us free from the law, or principle, of sin and death. What the Jewish Law was unable to do—give us life—God has now done in the person of his Son. By his oneness with our condition, sin has been dealt with (vv. 2–4). So we now live according to a new principle, in a new sphere, on the level of the spirit, instead of the flesh (NEB 'lower nature'—an unhelpful translation); there are two ways to live—the old way, dominated by selfish desires (i.e. the way of Adam), and the new, dominated by the spirit (vv. 5–8). It is difficult to translate the two Greek words for 'flesh' and 'spirit' without giving a false impression; Paul is not thinking of what came to be known later as the 'sins of the flesh', nor of piety, but of two possible ways of living; 'flesh' is what links man to the animal world, 'spirit' is what links him to God—cf. the notes on Galatians 3.

We know that we are living 'on the spiritual level' because the Spirit of God himself lives within our hearts—'the Spirit of him who raised Jesus from the dead', and has made us share in the same new life (vv. 9–11). Our old 'life' is dead, put to death with Christ, and has no more claim on us (vv. 12–13). We have passed from a condition of slavery to the status of sonship, and the proof of this is that we have received the Spirit of the Son, and we use the very word which Jesus used in addressing God—'Abba', i.e. 'Father' (vv. 14–16). Paul is here taking up the idea which he used in Galatians 4, and he continues it in v. 17, with the idea that sons are also heirs. Our sonship and our inheritance are always dependent on the fact that we are linked to him; at present we share his sufferings—and at the end we shall share his glory. Just as the whole of creation has been in bondage, sharing in the bondage of man, so now the redemption of creation is in sight; when mankind is finally set free, and enters into the freedom and glory which God intended, the universe, too, will become a glorious place. At present we see only the beginning of this process, and (as in childbirth) we are conscious of the present pain, but this is a guarantee of what is to come (vv. 18–25). In linking together the redemption of man and creation, Paul is using typical Jewish ideas about the End; with the fall of Adam, creation was put in bondage (Gn. 3.17); but when God redeems his people, creation, too, will be restored to the original purposes of God (e.g. Isa. 55.12–13).

So the Spirit is now at work within us, helping us even in our prayers (vv. 26–7). We may therefore be confident that in

162

every circumstance God is able to work for good. For God's plan for us goes back to all eternity: he knew us before we existed, and ordained that we should be made like his Son ('conformed to his image', who is the image of God); he called us, justified us, glorified us—the outcome is so certain, that Paul is able to use the past tense ('he has given his splendour') for what still lies in the future (vv. 28–30). Note that Paul speaks only of those whom God has foreordained for glory, and the working-out of his original purpose for Adam; he does not speak of predestination to destruction.

Since God is working his purpose out, there is nothing for us to fear; the gift of his Son for us is a guarantee that he will give us all things. No one can accuse us, since God himself pronounces our acquittal, and Christ is our advocate (he who died but has been raised from the dead). Nothing, therefore, can separate us from the love of Christ; neither human suffering nor the spiritual forces which are said to have mankind in their grip; the victory belongs to Christ. Note how, in this chapter, Paul speaks both of the Spirit of God and of the Spirit of the Son, of Christ living in us, and the Spirit living in us; Paul is describing an experience, not working out trinitarian doctrine, and he uses the different terms accordingly.

In chs. *9–11*, Paul deals with a problem that was of great importance to him as a Jew: what has happened to God's plan for Israel? Why, since he chose her to be his nation, and revealed himself to her, has he allowed her now to reject the Messiah? His anguish over this problem, and his sorrow that those to whom God gave everything should now stumble, are set out in *9*.1–5. Paul refuses to allow that the promise of God should have proved false: the promise to Abraham must stand firm—·but it has been fulfilled in those who are not his natural offspring; throughout Israel's history, argues Paul, God has always worked through those whom *he* has chosen; and now he has chosen to justify Gentiles, and not Israel (vv. 6–33). Paul, however, has not abandoned his prayer for Israel (*10*.1–4); the trouble with his people is that their zeal is ill-informed, and that they have pursued their own way of righteousness (a legal one) instead of God's way (the way of faith). The gospel has been preached to them, and they have rejected it (*10*.5–21). But Paul cannot believe that God has finally rejected his people—the very fact that he, Paul, is a Jew is proof that God has not done so, since Paul, together with other Jewish Christians, form a 'remnant', like the remnant of 7,000 men who remained faithful to God in the time of Elijah (*11*.1–6). Because of Israel's failure to accept the Messiah, God has turned to the Gentiles, and the gospel has been preached to them; and Paul believes that when they see what is happening, the Jews will in turn accept the good news (vv. 7–12). But the Gentile Christians must take heed—if God lopped off dead branches from the tree of Israel, and grafted in branches from a 'wild' tree, then there is nothing to prevent him lopping them off in turn, if they prove dead, and grafting back the old branches if they show signs of life again! (vv. 13–24). They must not be complacent: even Israel's present blindness is part of God's plan, and his promises cannot fail; when the Gentiles have fully responded to the gospel, then the whole of Israel will be saved (vv. 25–32). The section ends with a statement that the ways of God are unfathomable (vv. 33–6).

The final chapters of Romans are concerned with ethical problems; we shall not look at these in detail, because in many ways they echo the teaching of 1 Corinthians. They form, however, an integral part of Paul's letter, and one should note the way in which Paul sees ethical behaviour as dependent upon the theological argument of the earlier chapters. Because of all that has been said '*therefore*, my brothers, I implore you by God's mercy to offer your very selves to him . . .' (*12*.1); because of what God has done, the Christian belongs wholly to God.

Colossians

The letter to the *Colossians* was written to a Christian community unknown to Paul, and founded by Epaphras (*1*.7). Paul seems to think there is some danger of them being led astray by men who insist on various regulations that sound like Jewish observances (*2*.16–23). The tone of the letter is quite different from that to the Galatians, and it therefore seems unnecessary to conclude, as many have done, that there was some kind of 'heresy' in the Colossian church; Paul would have written much more sharply had this been the case. It is possible, however, that Paul is deliberately stressing the supremacy of Christ to various spiritual powers that the Colossians still regarded as influential; these would have been the astral powers which, according to pagan belief, dominated the destiny of men, and which have reappeared in recent times in the Zodiacal signs, believed by the superstitious to govern their destiny.

This theme of the supremacy of Christ is summed up by Paul in *1*.13–20. In vv. 13–14 Paul explains that God has rescued us from the old realm in which we lived and brought us into the kingdom of his Son; the imagery here is of light (v. 12) and darkness (v. 13), but it expresses what in Romans was put in terms of life and death. It is possible that vv. 15–20 are a 'hymn'; certainly they fall into two sections, and there is much parallelism and repetition. In the first 'verse' we are told of Christ's relation to creation. He is the 'image of the invisible God'—words that remind us of Adam, and the fact that he was meant to rule over creation as God's representative. As the image of God, Christ shows us both what God is like and what man is meant to be. This phrase also echoes words used about wisdom in Wisdom *7*.26—she is said to be the image of God's goodness—and the role that Christ is said to play here as the agent of creation is reminiscent, too, of what is said about Wisdom (as God's master-workman) in the book of Wisdom and in Proverbs *8*. Christ is supreme over creation—everything was created through him (including the spiritual forces that the Colossians fear), and everything has its meaning and existence through him; he is before and above everything (vv. 15–17). Similarly, Christ is supreme over the church—he is its head. He is the 'firstborn' of the dead—not simply the first to be raised, but the one who, according to Jewish custom regarding the firstborn son, has authority over those who follow him. God is fully present in him; and just as all things were created through him, so now all things are reconciled to God through him (vv. 18–20). The NEB translation does not bring out fully the remarkable and obviously deliberate parallelism between the two sections. We find the same words being used in both, even down to the prepositions ('In . . ., through . . ., unto . . .'). Christ is said to be 'firstborn' (i.e. first in time and status) in relation both to creation (v. 15, paraphrased in NEB as 'his is the primacy over all created things') and to the church. In these verses we see the development of ideas that we have met elsewhere in Paul's letters: in Christ, the purpose of God has its fulfilment and reaches its goal, and creation, as well as mankind, is renewed (cf. Rom. *8*); all things are reconciled to God through Christ, and so the existence and coherence of the universe, as well as the church, depends upon him. Paul's language here reflects the belief that creation itself had 'fallen' into corruption and incoherence, and therefore needed, like mankind, to be restored. We see another development in the idea that Christ is the head of the church which is his body, and so supreme over it; cf. 1 Cor. *12*.12–27 and Rom. *12*.4 f.

As in other Pauline letters, the practical outcome of belief is emphasized. We find this being done, e.g., in *3*.1–17. Here we are told that, since we have been raised to life with Christ, and since he is exalted to God's right hand, our lives are now 'above', hidden in Christ, and our thoughts should be centred 'above' (vv. 1–4). It is clear from the rest of the chapter that Paul is not here advocating heavenly meditation divorced from earthly realities. What he means is that we have exchanged the old existence for the new, and we should behave like it; it is once again the contrast between Adam and Christ—or, as Paul puts it here, between the old man and the new (vv. 9–10), paraphrased in NEB as 'the old nature' and 'the new nature'. The new man is 'being constantly renewed in the image of its Creator'—and we remember that in Col. *1*.15 Christ is the image of the invisible God; once again we have the idea that, in Christ, man is being made into what God intended him to be from the creation. Verses 5–8 describe what the life of the old man is like—the life that Christians have put off; vv. 12–14 describe the character of the 'new man' that they are putting on. And because there is one new man—Christ—there can be no division (v. 11). They must be united by love (v. 14); they form one body, and they must build one another up; whatever they do must be in the name of the Lord Jesus, and to the glory of God (vv. 15–16).

Ephesians

The letter to the *Ephesians* uses and adapts many phrases from other Pauline letters, and in particular there are a great many echoes of Colossians; words and ideas which we have met in Colossians reappear here. This is one reason why many scholars believe that Ephesians was written by someone who knew and admired Paul, rather than by Paul himself, and that it is an attempt to sum up Paul's teaching. The thanksgiving, in vv. 3–14, sums up the meaning of redemption; notice that it looks backwards, to the time of our election—'before the world was founded' (v. 4)—and forwards, to the time when we shall enter fully into our heritage (vv. 13–14). Everything happens 'in Christ'—our election (v. 4), our acceptance as sons (vv. 5–6), our redemption (v. 7), the gifts which God has given us (vv. 3, 9), including our share in the inheritance (v. 11). The Spirit has been given to us as a guarantee or pledge of what is still to come (vv. 13–14). Notice that God is the author of what happens, Christ the one through whom it takes place, and that the Spirit is received by the believer; this is not in any sense a trinitarian formula, but expresses an experience—which is how Christian doctrine develops.

The phrase 'you too' in v. 13 probably means 'you Gentiles' (i.e. as well as the Jews). This theme is taken up again in 2.11–22. After 2.1–10, where the readers are reminded that once 'you were dead' (as 'we' were), but have been raised with Christ, it is said that once they were strangers, non-Israelites, outside the covenant and promises of God (vv. 11–12). But now—in Christ—they have been brought into the circle of God's people, and made members of his nation; this has come about because in Christ there is no division, just one new man, and there is no longer any distinction between Jew and Gentile. The dividing wall between them has been broken down; this dividing wall is said to be the Law, which kept Israel separate from her neighbours, but perhaps it

167

refers also to the wall in the Jerusalem temple, beyond which no Gentile might venture on pain of death; now the wall is down, and both Jew and Gentile may enter into God's presence (vv. 13–19). The idea that they are 'members of God's household' leads into the picture of the Christian community as a building which is also the temple of God (vv. 20–2; cf. 1 Cor. 3.10–17).

The picture of the Christian's armour, in 6.10–20, reminds us that though Christ is greater than supernatural powers, and has won a decisive victory over them, they are still active; the Christian community must be prepared to meet them in the power of the Lord.

See the notes on these epistles in *Groundwork* 37a–c, o–p, k–l.

Suggestions for further reading

C. K. Barrett, *Reading through Romans* (SCM).
J. A. T. Robinson, *Wrestling with Romans* (SCM).
J. L. Houlden, *Paul's Letters from Prison* (SCM).
F. F. Bruce, *Ephesians* (Pickering and Inglis).

Chapter 10

Letters from other Leaders

Passages for special study:

Hebrews *1*.1–5; *2*.10–18; *4*.14–*5*.10; *7*.26–*8*.6; *9*.11–14, 23–8; *10*.1–25; *11*.1–3.
James *2*.
1 Peter *1*.1–*3*.12; *4*.12–19.
1 John.
1 Tim. *3*.14–16.
2 Tim. *2*.1–15; *4*.1–8.

ALTHOUGH the letters written by, or attributed to, St. Paul, make up one-quarter of our New Testament, he was by no means the only leader in the early Church to write pastoral letters to his congregations. It is perhaps a little unfair to include all of them in one study, as though they were also-rans, but since space is limited we are obliged to take them all together.

Hebrews

The longest of these, although it is headed in our translations, 'The Letter to the Hebrews', is not really a letter at all. It is true that it ends like a letter, but its beginning is quite unlike one, and it does not include any of the personal details or references to particular circumstances which one would expect in a letter. It is much more like a homily than a letter.

169

Notes on passages for special study

Hebrews begins with an impressive statement of the superiority of Christ to all previous revelations. In the past, God had spoken to his people through the prophets, but now he has spoken through his Son, so that the partial has been replaced by the perfect (*1*.1–2). The language used to describe the Son in vv. 2–3 echoes language which is used in Jewish Wisdom literature of the figure of wisdom (cf. Prov. *8*.27–30 and Wisd. *7*.25 f.). Similar ideas and language are found in Col. *1*.15 ff. and Jn. *1*.1 ff. This 'wisdom'—expressing the purpose of God—is embodied in the person of Christ, who is now enthroned at God's right hand, far above the angels (v. 4). Notice how this last verse introduces the main theme of Hebrews—the way in which Christ's death has dealt with human sins. But before the author explores this idea he is anxious to establish that Christ is superior to the angels. Christ has been given a 'superior title' to theirs—that of 'Son' (v. 5). In the rest of ch. *1*, he backs up the supremacy of God's Son with a number of Old Testament quotations.

Although the Son is superior to the angels, however, he was 'for a little while made lower than the angels' (*2*.9, quoting from Ps. *8*.5). In *2*.10–18 the author explains why. It was, he says, fitting that the Son of God should share human experience to the full. It was by sharing their suffering that he has been able to 'bring many sons to glory'; it was by sharing human nature and experiencing death that he has been able to deliver men from the fear of death. We find here an idea which we met in the letters of Paul: by sharing fully in human nature, the Son is able to 'sanctify' men and women and make them, also, 'sons' of God (vv. 10–11). Having experienced human weakness himself, he is ideally qualified to act as a priest on their behalf. It is this theme of the priesthood of Christ which is explored in later chapters, and which is the distinctive note in Hebrews.

Meanwhile, however, the author continues with the theme of Christ's superiority. We know already that Christ is greater than the angels, through whom, so it was believed, God delivered the law to Moses (cf. *2*.1–4). Now, in *3*.1–6, we are told that he is greater than Moses himself. Both of them were faithful, but Moses was only a servant, whereas Christ is a Son. This means that Christians, having received a greater calling than their 'fathers' (i.e. the Israelites), must be the more careful not to fall away (3.7–4.13).

In 4.14 the author picks up the theme of Christ as our great high priest. Jesus, the Son of God, has passed through the heavens to the throne of grace: i.e., by his death and exaltation he has come into the presence of God. He is able to act as a priest because he is able to sympathize with our weakness to the fullest extent, having himself been subjected to every kind of temptation, yet without sinning (4.14–16). This idea is spelt out in 5.1–10. Other high priests have been able to sympathize with their fellows since they themselves are 'beset by weakness'. But this meant that they had to offer sacrifices for their own sins, as well as for those of their people (vv. 1–4). Christ, however, though he experienced suffering in the days of his flesh, 'learned obedience through what he suffered' and was 'made perfect', so that he became the source of 'eternal salvation' to others (vv. 7–9). Unlike other high priests, he is a 'high priest after the order of Melchizedek' (vv. 5–6, 10).

This notion of a 'high priesthood after the order of Melchizedek' is, as the author himself admits, 'hard to explain' (v. 11). If it was difficult for his original readers to grasp, it is certainly obscure to us! What he is trying to do is to demonstrate the superiority of Christ to Jewish high priests. He does this by assuming that Ps. 110.4 refers to Christ (5.6), and then arguing that Melchizedek (who according to Genesis was priest in Jerusalem in the time of Abraham) was greater than the high priests who came from the tribe of Levi. The author of Hebrews believes that the superiority of Melchizedek is demonstrated in the fact that Abraham (the ancestor of Levi) gave a tenth of all he had to him (Gn. 14.18–20). Melchizedek appears only here in the New Testament, but it is interesting to find his name in some of the material from Qumran: perhaps he was a well-known figure in first-century Jewish thought. If Abraham paid a tithe to Melchizedek, this means that Christ, who is (according to Ps. 110) high priest in succession to Melchizedek, is greater than all the Levitical priests descended from Abraham; moreover his office, unlike theirs, lasts for ever (7.1–25). The argument reaches its conclusion in 7.26–8: since Christ is a perfect high priest he has no need to offer sacrifices for himself, and the sacrifice which he offered for others was made once and for all, when he offered up himself.

In order to understand this author's argument we have to realize that he is influenced by the Platonic notion of heavenly realities and earthly copies. He is therefore able to present Christ as the perfect high priest who functions in a heavenly sanctuary, the Jewish high priests as imperfect and temporary, serving in an earthly temple which is a copy of the heavenly one. Christ is a high priest who ministers in 'the true tent' or sanctuary (8.1–2), whereas the Levitical priests 'minister in a sanctuary which is only a copy and shadow of the heavenly' (v. 5). Indeed, we read in Ex. 25 that Moses erected the tent in the wilderness in accordance with a heavenly pattern which had been shown him on Mt. Sinai: it is this heavenly sanctuary in which Jesus is high priest. Similarly, the covenant which is established through Jesus is greater than the covenant established through Moses (8.6–13).

If the earthly sanctuary and priests are copies of the heavenly, so too is earthly worship. In 9.1–10 the author describes the layout of the sanctuary, and explains how the high priest enters into the Holy of Holies only once a year, there to make an offering for himself and the people. But Christ has entered into the heavenly Holy Place 'once and for all', making the perfect sacrifice with his own blood (9.11–14). The author has in mind here the ritual of the Day of Atonement. In the next paragraph he switches metaphors, and compares Christ's death with the sacrifice which sealed the covenant made on Sinai (vv. 15–22). Then he returns to the imagery of the Day of Atonement once more. If the 'copies of the heavenly things' needed purification with sacrifices, the heavenly reality itself clearly needed a better sacrifice (v. 23). Christ has entered into this true sanctuary, i.e. into heaven itself, into the presence of God (v. 24). He did not need to offer himself repeatedly, but 'once and for all'. In dying, he dealt with the sins of many—i.e. the sins of mankind (vv. 25–8).

The logic of all this is spelt out in *10*.1–18. The Law contains only a shadow of the good things to come: this is why it could not provide a final and perfect sacrifice (vv. 1–3). But what could not be done by animal blood has been done by the self-offering of Christ (vv. 4–10). So whereas the priests in the temple offered sacrifices every day of the year, Christ offered one perfect sacrifice, and then took his place at the right hand of God, as Ps. *110*.1 says (vv. 11–13); they stood, but he sat down, because his work was complete. By that one offering he sanctified his people for all time, so that there is no need for any further sacrifice (vv. 14–18).

So Christians may boldly enter the sanctuary; the barrier which kept men out of the Holy of Holies in the earthly sanctuary is a barrier no longer, for Christ has entered into the presence of God, and opened up a way for us to enter. The Law once provided rites of purification for those who were unclean; now we have been made clean by being sprinkled with Christ's blood and washed in baptismal waters (vv. 19–22). So we must hold fast to the confession of this hope, helping one another and encouraging one another (vv. 23–5). Chapter *10* ends with a warning not to fall away (vv. 26–39).

In ch. *11* we have a famous roll-call of Old Testament heroes who are held up to us as examples of those who had faith. This author's understanding of the term 'faith' is not quite the same as Paul's, though of course their ideas overlap to some extent. Whereas Paul thinks primarily of a personal relationship with God, the author to the Hebrews understands faith in terms of confident hope: faith is for him a conviction about unseen realities, and confident hope of future salvation (*11*.1–3). This is why some of those whom he lists in the rest of the chapter are not always those whom we most naturally think of as examples of faith. With their example to encourage us, we must persevere in the same 'race', keeping our eyes fixed on Jesus, who has gone before us; he is the supreme example of faith, for he endured shame and suffering in sure hope of the goal before him (*12*.1–2). Christ's example should encourage us not to slacken (v. 3).

The theme of perseverence is explored in various ways in the final chapters, until the concluding benediction and greeting (*13*.20–5).

James

The epistle of James is another homily which has the appearance of a letter; this time the only personal note is found in the greeting in v. 1. The contents are almost entirely moral exhortation, and there is very little in it which is specifically Christian. The writer is soaked in the Old Testament, and he writes to the 'twelve tribes dispersed throughout the world', i.e. to Jews outside Palestine. Tradition has assumed that he was James the brother of the Lord, but he does not claim this, and James was a common name.

Notes on James 2

1–7. *Snobbery*. James urges his readers to avoid snobbery. In all communities, there is a tendency to give special privileges to those who already possess them, and to despise those who have nothing. But these worldly distinctions are of no account. Verse 5 reminds us of the Beatitudes (cf. Lk. *6*.20–1), and also of some of Paul's teaching (cf. 1 Cor. *1*.26–9; 2 Cor. *6*.10). Servile behaviour towards those with money is the more absurd, since it was often the rich who oppressed members of the Christian community (vv. 6–7).

8–13. *The Law*. The attitude of the community towards the poor is not in keeping with the command given in the Law to love one's neighbour as oneself (vv. 8–9). Failure to keep part of the Law cannot be excused on the grounds that one has kept the rest of it (vv. 10–11).

14–26. *Faith and works*. It is sometimes assumed that James' teaching here is meant as a direct denial of Paul's doctrine of justification by grace through faith. What James is attacking, however, is a distortion of Paul's teaching, if indeed it owes anything at all to Paul. It may be that what he has in mind is the 'antinomianism' which is a complete misunderstanding of Paul's position, and assumes that liberty from the Law means licence to behave as one wishes. James is protesting against those who claim to believe, but show no evidence of this belief in their lives. Paul is equally insistent that Christian faith should bear fruit in Christian actions. The differences between the writers are partly due to their different use of words. For Paul, 'faith' is primarily a personal trust in God, and in what he has done, whereas the example which James gives of faith in v. 19 shows that he understands the term to mean the acknowledgement of what is true. 'Works' for Paul means the works of the Law, by which man foolishly tries to justify himself, whereas James uses the term of the actions which issue from faith. But their differences are also due to their very different approaches. It is not so much that James is here deliberately contradicting Paul, as that he sees religion in a different way: for him, faith in God is expressed primarily in moral action. So to him the story of Abraham (vv. 21–4), which for Paul was an example of justification by faith, demonstrates the principle that faith alone is insufficient.

1 Peter

Scholarly opinion is divided between those who believe this letter to have been written by Peter (or at Peter's behest), and those who believe it to be the work of a later author, writing in Peter's name. See *Groundwork* 38f. It is addressed to Christians who are threatened with persecution, and encourages them to stand firm in the face of suffering. But the earlier part of the letter includes advice about everyday conduct in more settled times.

Notes on passages for special study

After the opening salutation (*1*.1–2), we have a prayer of thanksgiving which serves to remind the readers of what God has done for them in Christ. Their hope for the future is founded on Christ's resurrection (v. 3) and is safe from all dangers (v. 4). They look for a future salvation (v. 5) and therefore rejoice, even though at present they may have to endure suffering (v. 6). This suffering will test their faith, as they wait for the final revelation of Christ and their own salvation (vv. 7–9). The Old Testament prophets spoke of this salvation, together with the sufferings and glory of Christ (vv. 10–12).

In view of the hope which is theirs, Peter's readers must behave in a way which befits obedient children (vv. 13–14). Since God who called them is holy, they must be holy too—an echo of God's call to Israel in Leviticus (vv. 15–16). They call God 'father', but they must remember that he is also judge (v. 17). The imagery of vv. 18–19 suggests both the purchase (or 'redemption') of a slave with money, and the redemption of the first-born with a lamb (Ex. *34*.20; cf. also the passover lamb, which redeemed the first-born at the Exodus, Ex. *12*.12 f.). It is through Christ that they have their hope in God (vv. 20–1). So they are to love their fellow Christians, since they have been born again through the word of the Lord, which is the word of the gospel (vv. 22–5).

As new-born infants, they must set aside all evil, and build themselves up on the pure milk of goodness (*2*.1–3). Coming to Christ, the 'living' stone rejected by men but chosen by God, they are to allow themselves to be built into a spiritual house, a temple; they are to be a holy priesthood, offering up spiritual sacrifices (vv. 4–5). Notice how, like most New Testament writers, this author moves easily from one metaphor to another. The idea of Christ as the stone is explored in three Old Testament quotations (vv. 6–8). The calling of the Christian community is spelt out in v. 9 in terms which were once addressed to Israel. As God's people, they are called to declare to others what God has done for them, in bringing them out of darkness into light. Verse 10 echoes Hos. *2*.23.

The next section of the epistle spells out the moral implications of the gospel. It is introduced by the general appeal in vv. 11–12. Then follows a command to obey the emperor, and those in authority (vv. 13–15) despite the fact that these powers may be antagonistic to the Church (see *4*.12–19); Christians are to live responsibly in society (vv. 16–17).

Slaves are to obey their masters, even when they are ill-treated; if they are punished unjustly and suffer this patiently, then they are following the example of Christ himself, who also suffered without retaliation (vv. 18–21). The thought of Christ's suffering is introduced here as an example, but leads quickly to the idea that his death resulted in our redemption (vv. 22–5).

Wives are to obey their husbands, and to behave modestly (3.1–6). But husbands, 'in the same way', are to treat their wives with consideration (v. 7). The whole community is to live in brotherly love and sympathy, a command which is backed up with a quotation from Ps. 34 (vv. 8–12).

4.12–19. At this point in the epistle, the author turns his attention to the imminent danger of persecution. It is a 'fiery ordeal' which tests them (v. 12). Nevertheless, they should rejoice that they have the opportunity to share Christ's sufferings; when his glory is revealed they will be overjoyed (vv. 12–13). There is a clear distinction between suffering 'as a Christian' and suffering as a wrongdoer (vv. 14–16). Persecution heralds the final judgement: if suffering comes now to the members of the Christian community, how much worse will be the punishment which comes to others (vv. 17–19).

1 John

Once again we have what is really a homily rather than a letter, this time without any conventional greetings at either the beginning or the end, and without any indication of authorship. Nevertheless, even though 1 John lacks the features of a letter, it is addressed to a particular community. It is a pastoral message to a group whom the author knows well. Its basic theme is very simple: it is that God is love. The author (by tradition named 'John') explores this idea, together with the truth which is dependent on it, namely that God's children are those who share his love. At the same time, he condemns those who show themselves to be liars, either because they do not believe the truth or because they do not love their fellow Christians.

177

1.1–4. *Witnesses to the word.* The author begins by reminding his readers that the gospel which they have believed was proclaimed to them on the authority of those who were witnesses of the ministry of Jesus. Notice how the terms he uses in v. 1 echo the language of John *1*.1 ff.: 'beginning', 'word', 'life'. This may well be deliberate. The author is anxious to emphasize the reality of what we call the incarnation. Fellowship with God is dependent, for this writer, upon belief in Jesus as his Son.

1.5–*2*.11. *Light and darkness.* John sums up his message as 'God is light'—another echo of John *1*.1 ff. (v. 5). This means that those who claim to have fellowship with him cannot walk in darkness: anyone who imagines that sin is compatible with Christian living is in error (vv. 6–7). Nevertheless, the author is bound to admit that in practice Christians do not live up to this ideal; though they walk in the light, they are still liable to sin. Anyone who claims that he is free from sin is also in error. For those who admit their sin, however, there is forgiveness through Christ's death (vv. 8–10). Placed side by side, these statements may seem contradictory, but they correspond with Christian experience. John is at one and the same time attacking two opposed erroneous positions—the ideas that sin does not matter and that Christians never sin. His own position is summed up in *2*.1 f.: they ought not to sin, but if they do they have both an advocate with God and an expiation from sin in Jesus Christ. The author then repeats his original statement that Christians ought not to sin. Those who claim to know Christ will keep his commandments; if they fail to do so, they are not speaking the truth (vv. 3–6). He realizes that he is repeating what they already know; the commandment is 'new' only in the sense that it is the 'new' command given by Jesus to his disciples (vv. 7–8; cf. Jn. *13*.34). Jesus is the true light, and those who belong to him must love their fellow-Christians; hatred belongs to the darkness (vv. 9–11).

2.12–17. *Appeal to the readers.* John addresses three groups—'little children', 'fathers' and 'young men' twice over. 'Children' is a term which he uses repeatedly throughout the epistle; 'fathers' and 'young men' may perhaps refer to officials within the community. The messages are appropriate to each group, and repeat what the author has already written, except that he mentions for the first time 'the evil one' or devil. If the evil one is opposed to God, so too is 'love for the world'. The author's attitude to the world seems very negative, but what he has primarily in mind are selfish attitudes—lust and greed—which are totally contrary to the love which stems from God.

2.18–27. Antichrist. John believed that the final day of judgement was close at hand. Following Jewish tradition, he expected opposition to God to reach its peak just before the end; this opposition is summed up in the figure of the 'antichrist' (v. 18). In fact, he says, there are already many antichrists here, in the form of false teachers. The Christian community he is addressing has already been split by heresy; those who remain are those who hold to the truth, and are faithful to the tradition which was given to them from the beginning (vv. 20–1, 24). Those who have left (v. 19) are those who have believed a lie: they do not accept Jesus as Messiah (v. 22). Since Jesus is Messiah, he is also God's Son, and any denial of the Son must be a denial of the Father, with whom he is one (vv. 22–3). John's readers have been 'anointed' (perhaps with the Holy Spirit) and this is why they should know the truth (vv. 20–1, 27): Jesus himself is the anointed one ('Messiah').

2.28–3.24. Children of God. Those who dwell in Christ will not be ashamed when he comes: since he is righteous, this means that they, too, must do what is right (vv. 28–9). Christians are children of God—and that means being like him (3.1–3). This is why those who truly belong to him do not sin; John once again attacks the false teaching that sin does not matter (vv. 4–7). Those who sin are children of the devil, not of God (vv. 8–10). So John returns again to the theme of love. Christians must love one another (v. 11). Cain and Abel are 'types' of those who hate and those who love. The former was a murderer and evil, the latter righteous (v. 12). But though

179

Christians (like Abel) are hated by the world, they have passed out of death to life (vv. 13–14). It is those who hate (like Cain) who dwell in death (vv. 14–15). Love is demonstrated supremely in Christ's death on our behalf; we ought to show similar love to our fellow Christians (vv. 16–18). Once again we have a criterion by which we may know that we belong to the truth: do we keep his commandments? (vv. 19–22). His commandments are to believe in Jesus Christ his Son and love one another (vv. 23–4).

4.1–6. The spirits of truth and error. Christians know that they belong to God through the presence of his Spirit (3.24). But there are other spirits. Those which are true confess that Jesus is the Messiah, and that as Messiah he had come in the flesh (v. 2). John seems here to be attacking a 'docetic' heresy which tries to separate the human Jesus from a supernatural Christ; those who held this view believed that the Christ had 'descended' on Jesus at his baptism and left him just before his death. (See *Groundwork* 37o.) John condemns this teaching as false (v. 3). Those who spread it belong to antichrist and to the world, not to God; they are led by the spirit of error, not the spirit of truth (vv. 4–6).

4.7–21. The meaning of love. Once again John returns to his main theme of love. God is love, and those who know him cannot fail to love others (vv. 7–8). The love of God is seen in the fact that God sent his only Son into the world as the expiation of our sins (vv. 9–10). This is why we must love one another (vv. 11–12). John goes over the same ground with monotonous regularity, so that one keeps thinking 'I've just read that!' In v. 13 we are told again that the presence of the Spirit is the guarantee that we dwell in God. John has borne witness to the truth that God has sent his Son to save the world, and the test of orthodoxy is whether or not one confesses Jesus to be God's Son (vv. 14–15). In him we see God's love, and so have confidence for the day of judgement, for love excludes fear (vv. 16–18). Because of his love we love him, but we cannot love him without loving our fellow-Christians also (vv. 19–21).

180

5.1–12. *Faith in Jesus.* The next paragraph continues the theme of love, but gradually concentrates on the importance of belief. Those who believe that Jesus is the Christ are all God's children, so that we cannot love the Father without loving them also (vv. 1–2). Those who are born of God love him and keep his commandments, and so overcome the world (vv. 2–4). It is our faith in Jesus as the Son of God which overcomes the world (vv. 4–5).

The next few verses are obscure, and have been the subject of much scholarly debate. It is at least clear that John is again concerned to emphasize that Jesus is the Messiah 'come in the flesh' (cf. *4.*2). Perhaps the most likely explanation is that the 'water' refers to Jesus' baptism and the 'blood' to his death. In other words, the Messiah (i.e. Jesus) experienced not only baptism (as the false teachers admit) but also death (v. 6). The Spirit of God witnesses that this is true (v. 7; cf. *4.*2). So there are three witnesses, says John—the Spirit, the water and the blood, and they agree (v. 8). This is a somewhat odd combination, and perhaps John is thinking of water and blood now as symbols of baptism and eucharist, in which case he has in mind three aspects of present Christian experience. The three witnesses all come from God, and may therefore be trusted. Together, they assure us that God has given us eternal life through his Son (vv. 9–12).

(The AV includes, as v. 7, a saying about three witnesses in heaven which is omitted from later translations. This is because they believe in God's Son they have eternal life (v. 13). They may be sure that they will be given whatever they latin translation of the epistle.)

5.13–21. *Conclusion.* The author assures his readers that because they believe in God's Son they have eternal life (v. 13). They may be sure that they will be given whatever they ask in accordance with God's will (vv. 14–15). So they should intercede for any Christian whom they see sinning; the 'deadly sin' is perhaps the false teaching which John has already condemned (vv. 16–17). Once again, John seems to contradict himself when he says that those who are born of God do not sin, but this is the ideal with which reality does not always correspond (v. 18): those who belong to God are totally opposed to the evil one (v. 19). John ends with a summary of the basis of his faith: Jesus Christ, the Son of God, has come, and through him we know God, who is truth and life (v. 20). So his readers must be on the watch against false 'gods' (v. 21).

The Pastorals

It may seem strange to return at this point in our study to letters which are attributed to Paul. However, the Pastoral epistles are so different in vocabulary, approach and atmosphere from all the other letters which bear Paul's name that it is generally agreed that they are among the latest documents in the New Testament to have been written. Moreover, their concerns are very different from the other 'Pauline' letters. They are concerned with maintaining true doctrine, with the ministry and with discipline within the Christian community, which is by now an established body. Most scholars believe that they were written by an unknown author in Paul's name, in an attempt to express what he felt Paul would have said to the Christian communities of the period had he still been alive. There are passages in the letters of a personal nature, and it may well be that our author included fragments of a genuine letter or letters from Paul.

Notes on passages for special study

1 Tim. *3.14–16. An early hymn.* The author's concern is with the way in which members of God's household should conduct themselves. The church is a 'pillar and bulwark of the truth' against all false teaching. As in 1 John, the question of distinguishing true doctrine from error has become an important one. 'Our religion' is summed up in a quotation from an early hymn or creed. It is about one who was 'manifested in the flesh' during his earthly life; 'vindicated' (the Greek word is one frequently used by Paul of Christian believers, and usually translated 'justified') in the Spirit—i.e. by his resur-

182

rection through the power of God's Spirit; he was 'seen by angels'—presumably at the ascension. He has been proclaimed among the nations, believed in throughout the world, and exalted in glory. The hymn emphasizes the universal acknowledgement of Christ. Contrast the hymn in Phil. 2, where Christ's humiliation during his earthly life is placed side by side with his exaltation.

2 Tim. 2.1–15. *Servants of the gospel.* The teaching which has been entrusted to Timothy must be passed on faithfully to others, who will be able to teach others in their turn (v. 2). As a soldier in Christ's service, he must expect hardship (v. 3); he must also be single-minded, and give his whole attention to the task in hand (vv. 4–6). These words are apparently directed to ministers of the gospel, who can expect to be provided for by the congregation (v. 6).

The command to 'remember Jesus Christ' reads strangely, but it is an appeal to take the steadfastness of Jesus in the face of suffering as an example (v. 8). It also serves to introduce a brief summary of the gospel which is reminiscent of Rom. *1*.3 f. Paul himself is a prisoner for the sake of the gospel; he puts up with hardship in order that others may be saved (vv. 9–10). Typical of the Pastorals is the quotation in vv. 11–13 of 'words which may be trusted', possibly another early hymn. The first two lines echo Paul's teaching about dying and suffering with Christ, and the saying about denying Christ reminds us of Mk. 8.38 and parallels. Timothy is to urge his congregation to be faithful to Christ; they should not waste time in arguments (v. 14). As for Timothy himself, he is to proclaim the truth in a straightforward manner, and prove himself worthy of God's approval (v. 15).

2 Tim. 4.1–8. *The end of the race.* Timothy is charged to be diligent in his task as preacher and pastor (vv. 1–2, 5). The warning about those who desert the 'sound teaching', although referred to as a further danger, undoubtedly reflects the situation in which the author finds himself (vv. 3–4). The final verses, on the other hand, sound like Paul's own words. He is at the end of his ministry, facing a martyr's death (v. 6).

Like a successful athlete, he has finished the race and looks forward to receiving the victor's crown (vv. 7–8).

Whether or not Paul did write these words, they are a fitting summary of his life and work.

Read the notes on these epistles in *Groundwork* 38 b–h and 37 s–t.

Suggestions for further reading

F. F. Bruce on *Hebrews* in *Peake's Commentary*.

L. E. Elliott-Binns on *James* in *Peake's Commentary*.

C. E. B. Cranfield, *I and II Peter & Jude* (SCM Torch Commentary).

C. E. B. Cranfield on *I Peter* in *Peake's Commentary*.

G. Johnston on I, II and III John in *Peake's Commentary*.

A. T. Hanson, *The Pastoral Letters* (Cambridge NEB Commentary).

Chapter 11

The Spiritual Gospel—St. John

Passages for special study:

John *1*.19–*3*.21; *4*.4–42; *5*.19–47; *6*.22–71; *9*.1–*10*.18; *11*.1–54; *12*.20–36 *13*.1–30; *14*; *15*; *17*; *18*.33–8; *20*; *21*.

WE have left the Fourth gospel until now, because it is clearly the work of a mature theologian reflecting on the gospel tradition after many years of Christian experience. It stands apart from the other three gospels, not only in content but in style and atmosphere, and it was for this reason that it was described as long ago as the second century by Clement of Alexandria, one of the early Church Fathers, as a 'spiritual gospel'. We must not make the mistake which has sometimes been made in the past, however, of assuming that when John differs from the Synoptics, it is because they are presenting 'facts' while he is presenting 'interpretation'. We have already seen how 'facts' and 'interpretation' are woven together in the Synoptic gospels, and the same is true of John. It is by no means certain that, when John differs from the other gospels over some detail, their version is to be preferred to his as historically more accurate. First, because John may sometimes be more accurate than they are. Let us take the so-called 'Cleansing of the Temple' as an example. John places this at the beginning of the ministry (Jn. *2*.13–22), while the Synoptics place it at the end (Mk. *11*.15–18 and parallels); it may well be that John's date, not that given by the Synoptics, is the 'correct' one. But secondly, we can see in this case how

185

unimportant the question of historical accuracy can sometimes be. The significant issue for all the evangelists is not the historical question 'When?' but the theological question 'What did it signify?' For Mark, the event was the final challenge of Jesus to the Jewish nation, and the symbol of the fact that God had rejected them because of their failure. For John, also, it is a symbol of Israel's rejection, but still more, it is a sign of Jesus' own death and resurrection, and of the way in which the Christian community is going to replace the old Judaism.

Read *Groundwork* 32.

The following is an outline of the gospel:

1.1–18	*Prologue* (see above, pp. 19 f.)	
1.19–51	*Introduction to Jesus*	
	1.19–34	The witness of John the Baptist
	35–51	The first disciples
2.1–*4*.42	*The beginning of signs*	
	2.1–11	The sign at Cana
	12–25	The Temple
	3.1–21	Nicodemus: Discourse on the signs
	3.22–*4*.3	John the Baptist
	4.4–42	The woman of Samaria: Discourse on true worship
4.43–*5*.47	*Signs of new life*	
	4.43–54	A dying child restored
	5.1–18	A paralysed man healed
	19–47	Discourse on life
6	*A sign at Passover*	
	6.1–15	Jesus feeds the crowd
	16–21	Jesus walks on water
	22–71	Discourse on the Bread of Life
7.1–*10*.21	*The Feast of Tabernacles*	
	7	Living Water
	8	Light
	9	The man born blind
	10.1–21	The good shepherd
10.22–*11*.54	*The Feast of the Dedication*	
	10.22–42	Jesus one with the Father
	11.1–45	Raising of Lazarus

Notes on passages for special study

1.19–34. The witness of John the Baptist. Notice how John tells us nothing about the message of John the Baptist, except the one significant fact that he was a witness to Jesus. Already in the Prologue we have had two references to this testimony of the Baptist (*1*.6–8 and 15). Now it is spelt out for us. When the religious authorities ask the Baptist who he is, his answers are negative: he is not the Messiah, nor Elijah, nor the coming prophet (vv. 19–21). When pressed for an answer, he declares that he is only a voice in the wilderness—the preparatory voice of Isa. *40*.3. But that means that the one who follows him must be the Lord: the stage is set for Jesus. Unlike the Synoptics, the Fourth gospel does not describe Jesus' baptism. Another important difference is that the Baptist is clear from the beginning about Jesus' identity, and makes this known to the crowds (vv. 29–31). The differences between the gospels offer us an example of the way in which incidents can be interpreted in the light of knowledge after the event. On this occasion, it is likely that Mark, who presents John the Baptist as being in the dark about Jesus' identity is closest to what we would term the historical 'facts'. But though the Baptist may never have recognized Jesus, nor have cried out 'Behold the Lamb of God', Christians looking back on John's life understood his message as bearing witness to Jesus. The words attributed to John acknowledge the superiority of Jesus. The significance of the term 'the Lamb of God' is uncertain; the Passover lamb, the lamb of Isa. 53 and the lambs offered in the temple to atone for sin have all been suggested as possible background ideas. Perhaps we should not choose between them, for one of John's themes is that everything in Jewish worship pointed forward to the coming of Jesus, and was made complete by his ministry and death.

The Baptist also claims to have seen the descent of the Spirit on Jesus (vv. 32–4), and explains the significance of this event as another witness to the identity of Jesus.

1.35–51. The first disciples. John repeats his witness to Jesus as the Lamb of God (vv. 35 f.), and two of John's disciples accept his testimony and follow Jesus. This is John's fate: the success of his mission is seen as men and women turn from him to Jesus (cf. *3.25–30*). One of the two— Andrew—immediately confesses to Peter his belief that Jesus is the Messiah (v. 41). This is a good example of the difference between John's understanding of Jesus and that of Mark: John assumes that the Messiahship of Jesus must have been obvious to the disciples, as well as to the Baptist, from the beginning of the ministry. By telling the story in this way, John makes the truth about Jesus clear to us, his readers.

Just as Andrew brought Peter to Jesus, so Philip, the next to follow Jesus, went in search of Nathanael. This time we are told that Jesus is the one foretold by Moses and the prophets (v. 45). The reference to promises in the Law as well as the prophets reflects Christian belief that the whole Old Testament pointed forward to the coming of Christ. Nathanael is sceptical, but a meeting with Jesus is suffcient to persuade him that Jesus is indeed the promised king of Israel. Jesus promises him that he will discover something greater than this—namely that Jesus is the Son of man who acts as the mediator between God and man (v. 51). The imagery and language are difficult for us to understand, but the main point which John is making is clear: the Baptist and the disciples alike confirm that Jesus is the one to whom both Law and prophets bear witness.

2.1–12. *The sign at Cana.* This incident is described by John as 'the first of Jesus' signs'. The term 'sign' is a characteristic word in the Fourth gospel, used to underline the significance of the miracles. In the Synoptics, most of the miracles are interpreted as signs of the inbreaking Kingdom of God. But for John, the miracles are explicitly Christocentric—that is, they reveal the truth about Jesus. Hence they are described as signs which reveal his glory. Another characteristic feature of the Fourth gospel is the series of discourses found in the mouth of Jesus. These, too, are essentially Christocentric, and are quite unlike the teaching found in the other gospels. The discourses spell out the significance of Jesus, and often use the same images as the signs.

In this story, Jesus responds to the need of his embarrassed host, but the somewhat harsh reply which he gives to his mother underlines his independence (v. 4): he acts when he thinks the time is appropriate, and not under any compulsion from others (cf. 7.1–10 and *11*.1–7). The six water jars have an enormous volume, but the exact quantity is unimportant; what is important is that the amount of wine provided is far more than is necessary, and of a quality superior to that which was drunk before. There are few readers of the gospel today who would want to take this story literally, and arguments about whether Jesus did or did not actually change water into wine distract us from the real point of the story. John's symbolism is clear. The water provided for the Jewish rites of purification is changed into the wine of the gospel by Jesus' presence. The Jewish system of worship points forward to Jesus, but it is replaced by him.

2.13–25. The temple. The same point is made by the next incident, which takes place in the temple at Jerusalem. This is not a miracle, and is not described by John as a sign, but its effect is very similar: it is a symbolic action performed by Jesus. Moreover, it points forward to a future sign—that of the resurrection (vv. 18 f.), Its meaning is spelt out in the conversation between Jesus and the Jews which follows. Once again, we see a difference in understanding between John and the Synoptics—an interesting example of the way in which a story could be used in different situations and be given different interpretations. Once again, in John, the story is given a Christological meaning. As in Mark, the action of Jesus points forward to the destruction of the temple—but it also points forward to the attempt of the Jews to destroy him. It is the temple of his body which will be destroyed and raised again. Like the story of the water changed into wine, this incident symbolizes the way in which Jewish worship (based on the temple) is replaced by the worship of the Christian community, which came into existence through the resurrection of Jesus.

3.1–21. Nicodemus. The first of the Johannine discourses takes the form of a conversation between Jesus and Nicodemus, a Jewish ruler trained in the Law. Before very long, however, we realize that the conversation is really between the Church and Judaism, and that the crucial point at issue is belief in Jesus. At the beginning of the chapter, Jesus addresses Nicodemus: 'Truly, truly, *I* tell *you*' (v. 3). The same words introduce plurals in v. 11: 'Truly, truly, *we* speak of what *we* know . . . but *you* (pl.) do not receive our testimony'. By the time we reach vv. 16 ff., we have the impression that it is no longer Jesus who is speaking but the evangelist, looking back on the coming of the Son of God into the world. We are very conscious, as we read these Johannine discourses, of the way in which incidents in the life of Jesus are being interpreted and made relevant to the life of the Church. We tend to think of 'interpretation' as something which we do to the biblical texts. But we see here how the process was already at work, during the period when the New Testament itself was being written. For John, the reaction of Nicodemus to Jesus symbolizes the reaction of the Jews of his own day to the gospel.

It is not surprising, then, if in this chapter we find language and ideas being used which mystify Nicodemus, and which he could hardly have been expected to understand at the time. According to John, Nicodemus fails to understand Jesus' words about entering the Kingdom of God. His misunderstanding is due to the fact that the Greek word translated as 'anew' or 'again' in our versions can mean not only 'a second time' but also 'from above'. Jesus teaches that one cannot see the Kingdom of God unless one is born 'from above', but Nicodemus, not realizing that the word is ambiguous, is puzzled by the idea of being born for a second time. The conversation is clearly artificial—Jesus and Nicodemus would not have conversed in Greek—but it serves to convey the idea of the inability of the Jews to grasp the truth.

Nicodemus represents the Jewish failure to understand the Christian gospel. He is no hypocrite; he respects Jesus, and he longs to see the Kingdom of God. But he cannot understand the relationship between the past and the present, between the old order of existence represented by Judaism, and the new. The birth which Jesus speaks of is spiritual, not physical, and the new order of existence belongs to the Spirit of God (v. 5). The signs which Jesus does (v. 2) are signs of this spiritual order, which is replacing the old order of Judaism.

Nicodemus, as a teacher of the Law, should understand this truth (v. 10). Yet is it not surprising if he fails to comprehend, for there is only one man—the Son of man—who has experience of the heavenly world (vv. 12 f.). This leads to the thought of his exaltation, and introduces a characteristic Johannine play on the meaning of the verb 'to lift up' (v. 14). Jesus was lifted up on the Cross; he was also lifted up in glory. For John, these are two aspects of the same thing: we shall find him, later, describing the crucifixion itself as the glory of Christ.

The coming of Christ demonstrates the love of God for mankind (v. 16). God's purpose is that the world should be saved through Christ's life and death. Notice how John has moved from the term 'the Kingdom of God' to the phrase which he prefers, and which conveys a similar idea—'eternal life'. Inevitably, however, those who refuse to accept the salvation which is offered, come under judgement (vv. 17 f.). To refuse the revelation of God which Christ brings is to reject the light and opt for darkness (vv. 19–21).

4.4–42. The woman of Samaria. This story offers the setting for a second discourse on a similar theme. Once again we see how a physical object can be a symbol of spiritual truth. The water of Jacob's well points us to the truth that Jesus is the source of 'living water'. Jesus promises that those who drink the water which he offers will never thirst again (v. 14). But we misunderstand Jesus' words if we take them literally; even he needs to ask for water to drink (v. 7). Like Nicodemus, the woman is unable to grasp that he is speaking in spiritual terms; when he promises living water he means not running water but water that gives eternal life. Like Nicodemus, she clings to the literal meaning of his words, and does not understand that they can be used as symbols of spiritual truth (v. 15).

The previous conversation is described as taking place at night with a highly respectable Jew. This one takes place in broad daylight with a woman (not the done thing) of doubtful reputation (v. 18) who was a Samaritan (with whom Jews did not mix, v. 9). She is at first sceptical about his claims: surely he cannot be greater than the patriarch Jacob (v. 12). The irony of her words for John lies, of course, in the fact that he believes that Jesus is indeed greater than Jacob. The woman is however impressed when Jesus demonstrates supernatural knowledge about her (v. 19). She therefore asks for his judgement on the question at issue between Jews and Samaritans: where is God to be worshipped—in Jerusalem or on Mount Gerizim? (v. 20). The answer is that soon neither place will be the centre of worship (v. 21). True worship is not tied to a physical place, but is spiritual, for God himself is Spirit (vv. 23 f.). Nevertheless, the Jews are nearer the truth than the Samaritans, for they know God, and salvation will come through them (v. 22). Readers of the gospel know that this salvation has come in Jesus, and that true worship is now focused on him (cf. 2.13–22). The woman guesses something of his meaning, since in v. 25 she speaks of the coming Messiah, and Jesus makes everything plain in v. 26 when he declares that he is this promised Messiah.

In vv. 31 ff. the theme moves from water to food. Just as Jesus has a supply of living water, so he has spiritual food (v. 32): this is nothing less than doing the will of God (v. 34). Once again, the imagery leads on to another idea. There are normally four months in Palestine between sowing and harvesting: but the time for harvesting is already here (v. 35). The disciples have been given the task of harvesting (v. 38). The Samaritans who come to hear Jesus are a sign of the coming harvest. After listening to Jesus they confess their own belief in him as the Saviour of the world (v. 42). The words are put into the mouths of Jesus' contemporaries, but they express the faith of the Church, several decades later.

5.19–47. *Discourse on Life.* After two more miracles or signs, we have yet another discourse. This brings out the significance of the miracles, in which Jesus has restored the life of a dying child and the paralyzed limbs of a sick man. Once again, physical things are taken as symbols of spiritual. The actions of Jesus are those of God himself (vv. 19 f.). This is why he is able to give life (v. 21). He is also entrusted with authority to judge (v. 22). The themes of resurrection and judgement belong together, since both belong to the End. But it is characteristic of John that he speaks of resurrection and judgement as both future (vv. 25–9) and present (v. 24). Those who hear Jesus' words have already passed from death to life (v. 24). But the dead *will* hear the voice of the Son of God and live (v. 25). Christians already experience eternal life—already know freedom from the fear of judgement and death, and the sense of victory over evil which are promised for the future. This sense of 'now' and 'then' is summed up in the typical Johannine phrase: 'the hour is coming and now is' (v. 25). For the believer, eternal life, the life of the Age to Come, has already begun.

Verse 30 repeats the theme of vv. 19–23 and introduces the

next theme, that of witness. The truth of what Jesus is and does and says is supported by various witnesses: it is supported by 'another'—i.e. God (vv. 32 and 37); by John the Baptist (vv. 33–5), by the works which Jesus himself does through the power of the Father (v. 36), and by the scriptures (v. 39). The Jews have neither heard nor seen the Father (v. 37)—words which remind us of what is said in *1*.18. They do not have God's 'word' in them, and that is why they do not believe Jesus, whom God has sent. The irony of the situation is that the Jews search the scriptures, which bear witness to Jesus the incarnate word. They expect to find eternal life there—and so they should, for they point forward to Jesus (v. 39). But they will not come to him and receive the life for which they are seeking (v. 40). These words clearly reflect a period later than that of Jesus himself, when the opposition of the Jews to the gospel has hardened. They have refused to receive Jesus (v. 43) and failed to recognize God's glory, revealed in him (v. 44). They have failed to understand the witness of Moses (vv. 45–7).

6.22–71. Discourse on the bread of life. The tradition in the Fourth gospel is usually quite different from that in the Synoptics, but in *6*.1–21 we have two stories which are already familiar to us. It is typical of John, however, that he follows these two incidents with a discourse which brings out their meaning for the Christian community. This time it takes the form of a conversation between Jesus and 'the Jews'. Once again, we can detect behind this conversation a debate going on in John's own time between the Church and the synagogue about the truth of Christian claims regarding Jesus.

The discourse is introduced by a paragraph explaining how the crowds went in search of Jesus (vv. 22–4). When they find thim, Jesus rebukes them (v. 26): they seek him because they ate their fill, and not because they saw signs—in other words, they did not understand the significance of what happened when Jesus fed them. The miracle is for them only a marvellous happening, not a sign revealing who Jesus is. Jesus once again points beyond what is physical to what is spiritual—to food which produces eternal life (v. 27). The next few verses play on the meaning of the word 'work'; the work required of the crowd is to believe in Jesus, but they want to see some work from him—some sign—which will persuade them to believe (vv. 28–30). Clearly they have *not* 'seen' the sign which Jesus has just performed! They challenge him to do what Moses did, and give them bread from heaven (v. 31). Jesus' reply is difficult, but it amounts to a contrast between the manna provided in the wilderness and the true bread which is given by the Father, and which provides life for the world (vv. 32 f.).

The crowd ask for this bread, but like the Samaritan woman in *4*.15, they are thinking in physical terms (v. 34). Jesus replies that he is himself the bread of life come down from heaven (v. 35). We have here the first of the great 'I am' sayings. (See *Groundwork* 32a.) Jesus himself is the full revelation of God, and provides spiritual food for the believer. The next few verses explore the meaning of the relationship between Jesus and those who believe in him (vv. 37–40).

The Jews take offence at Jesus' claims. They think they know where Jesus comes from—and it is not from heaven (vv. 41 f.). Once again, they are thinking on a physical level, while Jesus is using everyday language to point to spiritual truth. By claiming to have come down from heaven, he does not mean that he has no human parents, but that he has been sent by God. If the Jews refuse to believe in him, it is because they have not learned the truth taught them by God (vv. 43–7). Jesus repeats his claim to be the bread of life, superior to the manna, and goes on to say that the bread he gives is in fact his flesh—a reference to his self-giving in death (vv. 48–51).

The Jews are even more puzzled by this statement (v. 52). The answer which Jesus gives explains that it is in the eucharist that men and women can feed on him (vv. 53–6). These words remind us of those spoken at the Last Supper in the other gospels, which are not recorded by John. In the form given here, they read harshly even to us, who are familiar with them. In the context in which John places them, they would have been not merely a 'hard saying' (v. 61) but quite unthinkable: Jews (who were forbidden by the Law to eat meat containing blood) could never have thought of *drinking* blood. The form of words is the result of later Christian reflection on the meaning of the eucharist. Jesus is the source of life for those who believe in him. He is greater than the bread which was given to the Jews in the wilderness (vv. 57 f.).

It is difficult for us today to follow all the arguments in this passage, because they reflect ideas which are no longer familiar to us, and follow the 'rules of debate' which were used by Jewish rabbis of that period in expounding scripture. What *is* clear to us, however, is that the claim being made for Jesus here is that he is the fulfilment of Old Testament promises, and that in him God is revealed more fully than ever before. We know that Jews sometimes interpreted the manna given in the wilderness as a symbol of the Torah or Law given to Moses. God's Law or word provided spiritual food for his people. The Christian claim is that the Law was not itself the true bread from heaven, but pointed forward to the living bread, namely Christ.

Knowing something about the background of ideas helps us to understand why claims about Jesus have been stated in the way they have. Whether or not Jesus himself preached on the theme of bread we do not know. What *is* clear is that the discourse in the form which John gives it reflects not only years of meditation on the meaning of Christ for the believer, but many arguments with unbelieving Jews. For them, it was a 'hard saying' to suggest that Jesus was greater than Moses, greater than the Law, greater than all they had known of God in the past (v. 60). It is not surprising if many of those who had flocked to Jesus found it impossible, in the end, to follow him (vv. 61–5). The particular belief which is said to cause difficulty is the teaching on the eucharist in vv. 52–9—teaching which again reflects Christian beliefs and experience. Had Jesus himself taught in this way, then certainly no one would have believed him or understood him. We need to remember that John has superimposed one picture on top of another. One is the situation of Jesus himself, preaching to his contemporaries, and finding his preaching rejected. The other is that of the author, preaching *about* Jesus, and reflecting sadly on the fact that the Jews have rejected the gospel. For him, Jesus was the revelation of God, the living bread from heaven who gave life to the world: it was natural for him to put into the mouth of Jesus the claims which Christians wished to make about him, and which they believed had been made implicitly in all that he had done and said.

John dates the feeding of the five thousand at Passover (6.4), and his next section at the feast of Tabernacles, which was held in the autumn (7.2). John seems to make these links with the Jewish festivals deliberately. Since he believes that the worship of the Christian community has replaced that which took place in the Jewish temple, he is naturally concerned to show how Jesus replaces and fulfils the Jewish religious festivals. The themes of the discourses are therefore appropriate to the festivals with which they are linked: at Passover, Jesus spoke about bread, and at Tabernacles he speaks about water (7) and light (8), both of which played a part in the festival proceedings.

9.1–41. *The man born blind.* In this chapter we have another miracle without any exact parallel in the Synoptics, though it reminds us of the story in Mk. 8.22–6. The disciples' introductory question reflects the harsh belief of the time, that suffering was the direct result of sin (v. 2). The reply of Jesus rejects this view; his words suggest that the man was born blind in order that Jesus might work a miracle, but what they mean is that the man's deformity presents a situation in which God's glory may be demonstrated. Clearly John understands this miracle, like the earlier ones, as a 'sign': Jesus is the light of the world (v. 5), and this is why he is able to give sight to a man born blind. The man's sight also symbolizes his faith in Jesus—a faith which grows throughout the story, until he finally confesses his belief in Jesus (v. 38). We are reminded of the way in which Mark placed his story of a blind man in Mk. 8 side by side with the account of the disciples' confession of faith in Jesus. Jesus is the light of the world, but the coming of light inevitably means judgement for those who reject it (v. 39). He gives sight to those who are blind, but those who thought they could see become blind, because they refuse to believe in him (vv. 40 f.). The trouble with the Pharisees is that they think they know the truth, which has been revealed to them through Moses (vv. 28 f.). But they are so hide-bound in their understanding of God's truth that they fail to see the evidence of God's activity, even when it takes place in front of their eyes (vv. 30–3). This is the truth which the 'blind' man grasps, and which they fail to see.

10.1–18. The good shepherd. This discourse introduces a new theme, that of the true shepherd of the sheep. It begins with a general statement about the relationship between the shepherd and his sheep (vv. 1–5); this is described as a 'figure', and is in some ways similar to the parables in the Synoptics. In vv. 7 f. the meaning of the imagery is explored. Jesus himself is the door (vv. 7 and 9); it is through him that men and women find salvation, and those who teach other ways are thieves and robbers (v. 8). He is also the good shepherd, caring for the sheep (vv. 11 and 14); the image of the shepherd is a familiar one in the Old Testament for the leaders of the nation. The references to 'hirelings' (vv. 12 f.) suggests criticism of the religious leaders, who do not care for the welfare of their flock. By contrast, Jesus lays down his life for the sheep (vv. 11 and 15). Jesus knows his own sheep, and there are others who do not belong to 'this fold'—a hint that the mission of Jesus extends beyond the Jews to the world of Gentiles (vv. 14–16). The final verses stress Jesus' freedom of action: he lays down his life in obedience to the Father's will, but no one constrains him to do so. He is in control of everything that happens to him, even his death (vv. 17 f.).

11.1–54. The Raising of Lazarus. The illness of Lazarus, like the affliction of the blind man, serves as a setting for another demonstration of God's glory in his Son (*11*.4). Once again, it is emphasized that Jesus is in control of the situation and acts when he wishes (vv. 3–7). The disciples are aware of the danger involved in going to Judaea, but Jesus replies that he must work while he still has opportunity (vv. 8–10). When Jesus says that Lazarus has fallen asleep, the disciples misunderstand him (vv. 11 f.). The imagery of sleep reflects John's own belief that for Christians, death is a sleep from which they will be woken on the Last Day (v. 13).

The conversation between Martha and Jesus points to the meaning of the story. Jesus' promise that Lazarus will rise again (v. 23) is understood by Martha in terms of the conventional Jewish belief in resurrection on the Last Day (v. 24), but Jesus replaces this with the declaration that he is the Resurrection and the Life (v. 25). It is through believing in him that men and women are given life, and they do not have to wait for the Last Day, since they experience this life now.

Like the other miracles, this one is understood by John as a demonstration of God's glory (v. 40) which leads men to believe in Jesus (v. 41). The idea that Jesus performed miracles in order to persuade men and women to believe in him is difficult, and is contrary to the teaching of the Synoptics, though we can understand how John, looking back on the ministry of Jesus, could interpret the tradition about his marvellous acts in this light. What is interesting is the way in which John once again uses the physical as a symbol of the spiritual, which is why discussions about whether or not the raising of Lazarus was historical miss the point. This story, like the miracles in previous chapters, is important as a symbol—a 'sign'—of the truth that it is through Jesus that men and women experience the power of God which brings life out of death.

11.45–54. Plot to kill Jesus. The raising of Lazarus, like all the signs, leads some to believe in Jesus; but others refuse to believe, and plot Jesus' death. So we have the irony that in giving life to Lazarus, Jesus seals his own fate. Another irony is found in the words attributed to Caiaphas: it is better for one man to die for the people, than that the nation should perish (v. 50). The evangelist points out that these words have been fulfilled in a way which Caiaphas could never have expected (vv. 51 f.).

12.20–36. The hour of glorification. The 'Greeks' (i.e. Gentiles) who came to worship at the feast and wished to see Jesus are representatives of the Gentiles who later believed in Jesus. After the introductory verses (20–2) they disappear from the story. If Jesus seems to ignore them and speaks here about his coming death, it is because it is through the Cross that he is going to draw men to himself (v. 32). It is only when Jesus is glorified (v. 23) that the Gentiles will be able to see him, as they request (v. 21). It is typical of the Fourth gospel that Jesus speaks here of his death as the hour of his glorification. For John, the shame and defeat of the Cross have been completely obliterated by the glory and victory which Christians have experienced through it. The paradox of the gospel is that the glory of God—i.e. the revelation of God's nature—is demonstrated supremely in the Cross of Jesus. By the death of Jesus, God is glorified (v. 28).

In the prayer of Jesus, we have an echo of the Gethsemane prayer recorded in the Synoptics (v. 27). In this gospel, however, the idea that Jesus might pray to be saved from this hour (the hour of his glorification) is immediately rejected: Jesus is fully in control of the situation. Moreover, John assumes that Jesus, being obedient to God's will, was fully aware of the way in which men and women would experience salvation through his death (v. 32). We see here an important shift from the Synoptic gospels, where Jesus says almost nothing about the significance of his death. It was a natural step, once the Church had come to believe that the death of Jesus was part of God's purpose of salvation, to assume that Jesus had shared this knowledge from the beginning. Yet in picturing Jesus as fully aware of events from the beginning, John loses the sense of the human Jesus, sharing our experiences of tragedy, perplexity and darkness.

13.1–30. *The feet-washing.* This supper is dated by John as taking place before Passover (v. 1, cf. *18*.28, and see comment above on Mk. *14*.12–16). The incident described here is not recorded in the Synoptics, and is interpreted in a typically Johannine way: just as the miracles are signs, so this is a symbol of Jesus' love and service for others, which are shortly to be demonstrated to the full in the crucifixion. This is why the feet-washing symbolizes the disciples' total cleansing (vv. 8–10). It is an 'acted parable' on a theme which is already familiar to us from Mk. *10*.42–5 and Lk. *22*.24–7. As well as pointing forward to the crucifixion, it sets before the disciples a pattern for the behaviour which is expected of them

(vv. 12–17). Interwoven into Jesus' words are prophecies of Judas' betrayal (vv. 10 f., 18 f., 21–30). Notice how John cannot believe that even the treachery of Judas was outside the purpose of God or the foreknowledge of Jesus. Not only does Jesus' action fulfil scripture (v. 18), but Jesus himself commands Judas to carry out his plan (v. 27).

14. Farewell discourse. This chapter sums up the main themes of the Farewell discourses. Jesus is leaving his disciples, but he will return (v. 3). The coming of Christ is pictured somewhat differently from the glorious parousia suggested by the other evangelists. Instead of the promise of a future triumph, the emphasis is on what, when John wrote, was already part of Christian experience. First of all, the disciples are to see Jesus 'in a little while' (vv. 18 f.): this seems to refer to the resurrection appearances. Jesus also promises that he and his Father will come and live with those who love him (v. 23)—clearly a reference to a spiritual experience rather than a physical manifestation. But Jesus promises also to send the Paraclete, or Spirit (vv. 15–17), who will in a sense replace Jesus (vv. 25 f.). This emphasis is consistent with the rest of John's theology: we have seen that, although he still speaks of the Last Day, he stresses also that eternal life can be experienced here and now. It would not be true to suggest that John replaces the future hope with this 'realized eschatology'; the two ideas are found side by side in his gospel, as different ways of expressing Christian experience.

The disciples have no reason to fear (v. 1). Jesus, whom they know, is himself the way to God (vv. 4–7). Jesus reveals God to them, since everything he says or does is in obedience to his Father (vv. 8–11). After Jesus is glorified, the disciples will be able to do even greater works than they have seen him do, and these will also serve to reveal God's glory (vv. 12–14). Jesus emphasizes that those who love him will keep his commandments (vv. 15, 21, 23 f.). It is to them that he will send the Spirit (v. 16); to them that he will show himself (v. 21); with them that the Father will dwell (v. 23). Notice the way in which Christian experience is here expressed in terms of Father, Son and Spirit. This is not a formal expression of

201

trinitarian belief, but we see how this develops out of Christian experience. The final paragraph of the chapter repeats the themes of the earlier verses.

15. The true vine. The image of the vine reminds us of the Synoptic parable of the vineyard (Mk *12* and parallels), but as usual in John, the image is applied directly to Jesus with the words 'I am'. In the Old Testament, Israel is described as a vine (e.g. Ps. *80*.8–16), but now it is Jesus himself who is the vine. Those who believe in him are members of the true people of God. The image of God as a vinedresser who prunes out useless branches reminds us of Paul's metaphor of the olive tree in Rom. *11*.16–24. For Paul, it is a warning to Israel; here it seems to be a warning to Christians who prove faithless (vv. 1–8). Once again, we are reminded that the sign of the disciple is that he keeps Jesus' commandments (vv. 6–11).

The command is to love one another, and their love is to reflect Jesus' love for them (v. 12). The meaning of that love is spelt out in vv. 13 ff. The argument reminds us very much of the teaching in 1 John.

In contrast to the love shown to one another within the Christian community, the disciples can expect to be hated by the world outside. They will be hated because Jesus himself has been hated; and in hating him, men are hating God, since Jesus has revealed God to them through his actions (vv. 18–25).

Nevertheless, the Spirit (v. 26) and the disciples (v. 27) both bear witness to Christ. The Spirit is described, as before (*14*.16 f.), as the Spirit of truth and as the Paraclete. This last word is translated as 'Counsellor' in the RSV and as 'Advocate' in the NEB. In Greek, the word means literally 'one who is called alongside', and is therefore often used of a legal advocate, offering counsel and support. But the Paraclete in John also teaches the disciples (*14*.26), bears witness to Christ (*15*.26), and acts as a counsel for the prosecution rather than the defence when dealing with the world (*16*.8–11).

17. Jesus' prayer. The Farewell discourses lead into this final prayer of Jesus, which sums up many of the themes of the gospel. The death of Jesus is the hour of his glorification, and the means by which he glorifies the Father (v. 1). It is through his death that men will come to know God, and so receive eternal life (vv. 2 f.). His death completes the task of revealing God to men (vv. 4 f.).

Jesus prays for his disciples, to whom he has revealed God's name—i.e. his nature and character (vv. 6 ff.). Jesus in turn, is glorified in them: that is, his work of bringing men and women out of darkness into light is continued in them (v. 10). Since Jesus is returning to the Father, the disciples will be left without him in the world (v. 11). He therefore prays for their protection (vv. 14 f.). Just as Jesus was sent into the hostile world, so now he sends them (v. 18).

The thought of mission leads to a prayer for those who will come to believe through their witness (v. 20). The unity of the Church is to reflect the unity of the Father and the Son (v. 21). The Church is to share also in Christ's glory (v. 22). The goal is that the world may believe (v. 23). The final prayer is that those who believe should be with Christ, sharing in God's glory and love (v. 24), since they have accepted the revelation of God in his Son (vv. 25 f.).

18.33–8. *The trial before Pilate.* With the story of the Passion (*18–19*), we find ourselves back on ground which is familiar to us from the Synoptics, though John follows his own tradition even here. One important difference, e.g., is seen in the last words of Jesus from the Cross in *19*.26–30.

In the Synoptic account of the trial before Pilate, Jesus refuses, after his initial response to Pilate, to make any further reply to him. In the Fourth gospel, however, the evangelist uses a conversation between Pilate and Jesus to bring out the truth about Jesus' kingship. Jesus' kingdom is not a political one (v. 36). He acknowledges that he is a king (v. 37), but immediately substitutes his own definition of his role: he has come to bear witness to the truth—that is to reveal God (cf. *1*.17). Pilate, confronted with the one who embodies truth, is nevertheless unable to see it, and breaks off the conversation with the unanswered question 'What is truth?'.

20. The resurrection. Like the Synoptics, John tells the story of the empty tomb (vv. 1–10), though his version refers to only one woman instead of a group. In this gospel, two disciples come to see the empty tomb. Like the signs and symbols in the rest of the gospel, the empty tomb points to something of far greater significance than the disappearance of a body. This is why John records the story of a disciple who 'saw and believed'. Whereas in the Synoptics the empty tomb does not create faith, for John it is a 'sign' that Jesus has been raised, and can be understood as such by those with eyes to see. Yet even for John, the account of the empty tomb needs to be supported by stories of what it symbolizes—namely the experience of meeting the Risen Lord.

It is remarkable that a woman is said to be the first to see Jesus after the resurrection (vv. 11–18). At first she fails to recognize Jesus—a reminder that the resurrection is not simply a restoration of Jesus to earthly life (v. 14). The command not to touch him because he is not yet ascended is puzzling (v. 17): how can he be touched *after* his ascension? The phrase used here actually means 'stop clinging to me', and suggests that Mary is thinking that everything is now as it was before the crucifixion; what she is clinging to is Jesus as she has known him up to now. Perhaps the command is intended to remind Christians of John's day that they should not long for the old days when Jesus was present in the flesh.

In the evening, Jesus appears to his disciples (vv. 19–23). According to John, it is on this occasion that the disciples receive the promised Spirit (v. 22) and are commissioned to continue the task of Jesus in bringing salvation and judgement to the world (v. 23). For the disciples, as for Mary, the resurrection means a new beginning: the task of Jesus is handed over to them.

A week later, Jesus comes again (vv. 26–9), and dispels the doubts of Thomas. On this occasion, Jesus invites Thomas to touch him, in contrast to his command to Mary; the suggestion that Jesus can be touched also seems strange in the context of a story in which Jesus is able to pass through closed doors (vv. 19, 26). If we try to tie up these details into a coherent picture we shall not succeed. Each of them is included in order to make a particular point about the Risen Lord. If he passes through locked doors, this demonstrates that he is no longer tied to a physical body; if he invites Thomas to touch him, this is to demonstrate the identity of the Risen Lord with the Jesus who had been crucified. But Thomas has no need to touch; his confession of faith is the climax of the gospel. He acknowledges that in Jesus he has met his Lord and God (v. 28): the promise of *14*.5–11 is fulfilled. Verses 29–31 remind us that we do not need to see what Thomas saw in order to share his faith.

21. Appendix. After *20*.30 f., ch. *21* reads like an addition. Some scholars have argued that it was not written by the author of the rest of the gospel, but this is by no means certain. The story is of another resurrection appearance to the disciples, this time in Galilee. The account of the large catch of fish resembles the story in Lk. *5*.4–7. In both gospels, the story is interpreted as conveying to the disciples the truth about who Jesus is. In John, the miracle is followed by a meal of bread and fish (vv. 9–14). In the early Church, bread and fish were symbols of the eucharist, and the first readers of the gospel would no doubt think of the occasions when they had been aware of the presence of the Risen Lord as they ate together. Many explanations have been given of the number 153, but we do not know what John himself understood by it: certainly it is likely that the huge catch of fish symbolizes the large number of men and women who would be brought into the Church as the result of the disciples' mission (cf. Mk. *1*.17).

In the conversation between Jesus and Peter which follows, however, the metaphor switches from fish to sheep. Peter is commissioned to care for Jesus' sheep. The threefold question is probably intended to reinstate Peter after his threefold denial of Jesus. By the time this story was written, it is likely that Peter had already been martyred (vv. 18 f.). As for the beloved disciple, he bears witness in another way: for it is he, we are told in v. 24, who has written these things, and his testimony is true. The final comment in v. 25, if taken literally, seems an absurd exaggeration. Yet its truth is that the work of Jesus in the world continues and knows no end.

Suggestions for further reading

A. Richardson, *The Gospel according to John* (SCM Torch Commentary).
* C. K. Barrett on *John* in *Peake's Commentary*.
* John Painter, *John, Witness and Theologian* (SPCK).
H. J. Richards, *The Miracles of Jesus* (Fontana).

Chapter 12

A Faith for all Times

Passages for special study:

Revelation *1*; *7*; *21*.1–*22*.5.

Read *Groundwork* 39 and 20 l.

THE book of Revelation is a strange and enigmatic book. Perhaps for that reason, it has fascinated many Christians, who have hunted through its pages trying to find hidden messages and prophecies about the end of the world. In some ways, this is an entirely natural thing to do, since the book is an apocalypse, intended to encourage faithful Christians by revealing to them what the author believed would soon take place, but concealing its message in bizarre imagery. Nevertheless, the attempt to find hidden prophecies about world history in the twentieth century (or any other century) is certainly a misunderstanding of what the author was trying to do. For in any attempt to relate his images to later historical events, it is only possible to make sense of them by reinterpreting them and reading new meanings into them. What the original author was concerned to do was to comment on contemporary events and encourage Christians of his time by describing the signs which would herald the final judgement and the blessings which would follow for the elect. We must recognize that in many ways he was mistaken: the end did not come when he expected. We do the author no service by suggesting that his 'prophecies' can still (with a little adjustment) be taken literally. The book's value in the first century

AD was as a message of encouragement to men and women who were being persecuted for their faith. If we are to find it of value in the twentieth century, we must 'demythologize' it, and understand it as a series of images representing Christian confidence in the love and justice of God and in the ultimate triumph of good over evil.

Notes on passages for special study

1.1–3. *Introduction.* John describes his book both as a revelation and as a prophecy. He believes that the events he describes will take place 'soon'. What he forecasts is the end of the present social order and the vindication of those who have been faithful to Christ.

1.4–9. *John's letter.* John's letter to the seven churches takes up the whole of Rev. *1–3*. After the description of his vision (*1*.10–20), we have particular messages to the individual churches, reproving and encouraging them. His introductory greeting describes God as the one 'who is and who was and who is to come (v. 4), words which echo Ex. *3*.14 but which also expand it. Instead of a reference to the Spirit of God, which is what we might expect today, he refers to 'the seven spirits who are before God's throne'. The number 7 signifies completeness, and recurs again and again in Revelation. Verses 5 f. pile up information about Christ, and some of the phrases which are used we have already met elsewhere—e.g. 'first-born of the dead' (Col. *1*.18; cf. 1 Cor. *15*.20); 'who loves us' (Gal. *1*.20) 'and freed us by his blood' (1 Jn. *1*.7), 'making us a kingdom of priests' (1 Pet. *2*.9). We are told that he is coming with clouds (v. 7)—an echo of Dan. 7.13, and a sign of his final victory. Those who once pierced him will wail—perhaps for him, perhaps for themselves; these words are an echo of Zech. *12*.10.

God himself is described as 'the Alpha and the Omega' (v. 8)—the letters at the beginning and end of the Greek alphabet. He is also 'the Almighty', a title used frequently in this book meaning the one who is in control of all things. John shares both the tribulation and rule which come from Christian discipleship (v. 9); he had probably been exiled to Patmos because of his Christian witness. He was 'in the Spirit', in a state of ecstasy, when he received the command to write to the seven churches (vv. 10 f., 19). The phrase 'the Lord's day' became later a common term for Sunday, the day on which Christ was raised from the dead, and probably has that sense here.

1.12–20. John's vision. John's vision is based on that of Daniel in Dan. *7.* In the middle of seven lampstands (representing the seven churches) he sees 'one like a Son of man' (v. 13; cf. Dan. *7.*13). His long robe and girdle suggest that he is dressed as a priest (cf. Ex. *28.*4), but they remind us also of the description of the angel in Dan. *10.5.* His head and hair (v. 14) are like those of the Ancient of Days himself (Dan. *7.*9), but his eyes and his feet are like those of the angel (Dan. *10.*6). His voice is described in a phrase taken from Ezek. *43.*2, and the sword from the mouth echoes Isa. *49.*2 (v. 16). According to Matt. *17.*2, the face of Jesus shone like the sun at his transfiguration.

Now the Son of man is described as the first and the last (v. 17; cf. v. 8 and Isa. *44.*6, *48.*12); he is also the living one, who is alive for ever, having conquered death (v. 18); this is why he controls the powers of death and Hades. The seven stars in his hand (vv. 16, 20) are said to be the angels of the seven churches, by which John perhaps means the heavenly representatives of the churches. We see how he uses a wealth of imagery, not always consistently.

7.1–17. The sealing of the saints. This chapter forms an interlude in the account of the opening of the seven seals on the scroll in heaven (chs. *5–6; 8*). The opening of the first six seals meant disaster and destruction; before the last one is opened—bringing even worse terrors—we are encouraged by a vision of final victory for God's people. So we have a momentary respite. The angels who control the elements held back the winds (v. 1), and the angels of destruction are told to stay their hand (vv. 2 f.) until the servants of God have been 'sealed' (a play on words) as his. It is clear from what follows

STUDYING THE NEW TESTAMENT

that they are not spared from physical suffering, so it must be against spiritual attacks that they are sealed. The idea of the seal on the forehead is probably derived from Ezek. *9*.4–6 (cf. also the Passover lamb in Ex. *12*). In *14*.1 the saints have the names of Christ (the Lamb) and of God on their foreheads. The number of the sealed is 144 thousand—i.e. $12 \times 12 \times 1,000$ (v. 4). The number 12 represents the tribes of Israel, and the square of that number (12×12) represents perfection. Multiplied by a thousand, we have a figure indicating completion. Christians saw themselves as members of God's people—belonging through Christ to Israel, even when they were of Gentile origin. So in spite of Jewish rejection of the Messiah, the number of God's people is complete. It is ironic that a symbol which was intended by the author to indicate a vast number was used by later Christian sects in an exclusive sense, and interpreted as meaning that *only* 144,000 people would be saved. The reference to a great multitude which no man could number' in v. 9 shows that the number is intended only as a symbol; there is no limit to the mercy of God.

The vision of vv. 9–17 looks beyond the terrible devastation which is going to begin in chapter *8* to the time of triumph. The 'throne' is the throne of God; 'the Lamb' is Christ, who has himself been sacrificed for mankind (cf. *5*.6, 9 f.). Both white robes and palm branches are symbols of victory. The multitude praises God for his salvation (v. 10) and the angels, the elders (cf. *4*.4: possibly Old Testament worthies) and the four living creatures (cf. *4*.6 and Ezek. *1*.5–14) all worship him (vv. 11 f.). Verses 13 ff. explain that the robes are white because they have been washed in the blood of the Lamb; i.e. the saints' victory and righteousness is due to his sacrificial death (v. 14). This is why they can stand in God's presence, and serve as his priests (v. 15). The images of v. 16 are familiar from the Old Testament, but some of them also remind us of phrases in the Fourth gospel (cf. Jn. *6*.35; *10*.11; *4*.10 ff.; *7*.38).

21.1–*22*.5. *The new Jerusalem.* John's final vision is of 'all things' made 'new' (v. 5). John is using here the familiar

210

Jewish idea of the renewal of creation. For him, however, as for other apocalyptic writers, the evil of the present order and the consequent destruction are so great that there is no continuity between old and new: there must be recreation, not mere restoration. John therefore sees 'a new heaven and a new earth' (v. 1; cf. Isa. 65.17 ff.); the sea—symbol of chaos and of all the powers of rebellion—exists no longer. The idea of a renewed or new Jerusalem (v. 2) is also found in the prophets (e.g. Isa. 65.18 ff.; 52.1) and in later Jewish writings, and the idea of a heavenly Jerusalem is used elsewhere in the New Testament (Gal. 4.26 f.; Heb. 12.22). With a typical mixture of imagery, Jerusalem is described as a bride, ready for her husband; the city is the dwelling place of God, so that the descent of Jerusalem from heaven fulfils the words of Ezek. 37.27. There are more echoes of Isa. 65 in v. 4 (cf. Isa. 65.19 and 17; also 25.8 and 43.18). It is God himself who commands all this, and his words are 'trustworthy and true' (v. 5); what he commands is already done (v. 6). The promise of 2 Sam. 7.14 is fulfilled for all who are faithful (v. 7), but those who prove cowardly and faithless in the face of persecution, together with all who practise evil, will be destroyed (v. 8).

Jerusalem—symbol of the Church—is now described as the Bride of the Lamb (v. 9). The image is used in the Old Testament of God and his people (Hos. 1–3; cf. also Eph. 5.25–30). John describes the glory of the city (vv. 11 f.). The number 12 reappears (vv. 12–14), now symbolizing not only the tribes of Israel but the 'apostles of the Lamb'. The measurements and adornments of the city (vv. 15–21) emphasize its perfection and glory. The twelve jewels mentioned remind us of the stones symbolizing the twelve tribes which were set in the high-priest's garment (Ex. 28.15–20), though the lists are not identical.

The city needs no temple, since God and the Lamb dwell in it (v. 22); nor does it need sun or moon, since the glory of God and the Lamb light it (v. 23; cf. Isa. 60.19). The city provides light to the nations (v. 24, cf. Isa. 60.3), and its gates are never closed, so that all may enter (vv. 25 f., cf. Isa. 60.11). Of course nothing 'unclean', that is not holy, may enter it (v. 27);

the author seems to have forgotten, momentarily, that he is describing a new heaven and earth in which nothing evil or imperfect can any longer exist.

The image of the river of life (22.1) is taken from Ezek. 47.1–12 and Zech. 14.8, and recalls also the river flowing from Eden in Gn. 2.10. The tree of life also comes from the story of Eden (v. 2; Gn. 2.9; cf. Ezek. 47.12). The opening words of v. 3 are a quotation from Zech. 14.3, and probably refer to the curse of destruction which overtook Jerusalem. The rest of the verse echoes Rev. 7.15, and v. 5 repeats 21.23. Like God himself, the saints will reign for ever and ever.

Diversity in the New Testament

The book of Revelation is very different in form and content from the other New Testament books which we have been studying. Nevertheless, in the three passages we have looked at we have frequently been reminded of ideas and expressions which we have found elsewhere. As we look back over the New Testament as a whole, we can see that there is a certain basic unity in what the various authors believe and say, but there is also considerable diversity in their understanding of Christianity and the ways in which they express their beliefs. There are as many approaches to the gospel as there are authors, even though on central questions their interpretations overlap. This is, of course, precisely what we would expect, since each author is writing from his own situation, expressing his own experiences, and reflecting the ideas and language of his own background. This means that attitudes to particular problems will vary according to individual circumstances. The book of Revelation provides us with a good example of this. The author has no respect for the Roman empire or its rulers. We have looked at passages where John describes the future happiness of God's people, but there are other passages where he describes the wickedness and punishment of God's enemies. In ch. 13–18 he describes Rome, first of all in terms of the beasts of Dan. 7, then as 'Babylon' (an earlier tyrant), and 'mother of harlots'. John exults in the certainty of the future destruction of Rome, her rulers and her empire. His approach is very different from that of Paul in Rom. *13*.1–7, who urges the Roman Christians to obey the government and all who were in authority. Whereas John thinks of Rome as an agent of Satan, Paul thinks of the Roman authorities as servants of God. Their different attitudes are due to their different situations. Paul, a Roman citizen, was writing at a time when the Roman empire was a power for law and order, and seemed to be on the side of the gospel; John, an exile for the sake of the gospel, was writing at a period when Rome had been ruled by a number of bad or mad emperors, and when the authorities had shown opposition to the Christian faith. It is important to remember these different circumstances if we are to understand the teaching of the various authors correctly, and this means, of course, that we cannot simply 'detach' the teaching from its original context and apply it wholesale to our own situation. Paul would have been astonished, for example, to find his teaching being used, as later happened, to justify the refusal of German Church leaders to oppose Hitler: he certainly was not thinking, when he wrote, of a situation in which rulers had become 'a terror to *good* conduct' (Rom. *13*.3), nor of one in which the Church itself had become so powerful that it was able to withstand evil rulers.

What we find in the New Testament, then, is far from being a systematic exposition of the Christian faith, or a ready-made stock of answers to all our problems. What we have is a series of documents, written by a number of men in very different circumstances, all of whom were concerned to relate their Christian faith to the situation in which they found themselves. The fact that the Church separated these particular documents from others, and made them the 'canon' of scripture, provided us with a body of material which sums up belief that 'God was in Christ' as nothing else could. Nevertheless, this has tended to obscure the fact that the original authors were totally unaware that they were writing 'scripture', and that they were concerned to express their own understanding of the gospel, and relate it to the particular circumstances of small groups of Christians for whom they had pastoral care.

The book of Revelation provides us with another example

of the diversity in Christian belief if we compare it with the Fourth gospel. Although it has sometimes been argued that these two books are by the same author, and although they often use the same vocabulary, they are very different indeed in atmosphere and emphasis. In Revelation, our attention is focused entirely on the future—on the blessings and rewards which lie beyond persecution and suffering. This is because the author is concerned to encourage those who are at the moment 'up against it'. He finds a meaning for the present distress in his hope for the future. In the Fourth gospel, on the other hand, the emphasis is very much on the present. Although the fulness lies in the future, 'eternal life' is something which is experienced here and now. Those who believe in Jesus already know what is meant by the promise that Jesus' words are satisfying food and 'living' water; already they walk in light, because they have the light of the world with them, and are cared for by the Good Shepherd. In other words, symbols which are used in Revelation to express the blessings of the future, are used in the Fourth gospel to express the blessings of present Christian experience. If we then compare these two books with the writings of Paul, we find that he sometimes emphasizes the one idea, sometimes the other. Perhaps this is because the needs of those to whom he writes differ, perhaps the explanation is that his own ideas developed. In either case, we see that the way in which the Christian gospel is expressed varies, according to the circumstances in which it is proclaimed.

Another example of the way in which the gospel can be expressed in different ways is seen in the different names which are given to Jesus. He himself, according to all four evangelists, referred to himself as 'the Son of man'. It seems unlikely that the Jews of the first century AD were expecting a leader who would be known as 'the Son of man'. However, the phrase would have said something very significant to anyone who was familiar with Dan. 7.13 ff. Yet the phrase meant nothing at all to those who were not familiar with its background. Even the title 'the Messiah' was little better. Of course it meant a great deal to Jews—though probably *different* things to different groups of Jews. But *Gentile* con-

verts to Christianity had never hoped for a Messiah: it was
hardly good news to tell them that they had one! So 'Christ'
the Greek form of 'Messiah', became little more than a proper name, and other ways of expressing faith in Jesus were used
—e.g. 'Jesus is Lord' or 'Jesus is the Son of God'.

In fact, Christians discovered a great many different ways
of expressing their faith and experience. Since the authors of
our New Testament books were Jewish, they most frequently
did this by taking over Old Testament ideas and phrases and
showing how Jesus 'fulfilled' them. The ideas are now so
familiar to us, and the phrases have become so much part of
our own vocabulary, that we tend to assume that they all
formed part of first century Jewish expectation about the
Messiah. We sometimes get the impression, from the way in
which we read the New Testament, that what the first Christians did was to look down a check-list of ready-made ideas
about what the Messiah would be like, and tick them off, one
by one. In fact, of course, as the general Jewish reaction to
Jesus shows, it was not nearly so simple. There was no ready
made 'glass slipper', waiting for Jesus to try on, and so prove
his identity. Rather, the New Testament authors, as they
attempted to explain their faith, took various ideas from the
religious experience of their people, and said: this term—or
that—is a way of expressing the impact which Jesus has made
on me; this idea—or that—is a way of describing what he has
done for my life. So we find them taking one word after
another—prophet, Messiah, priest, shepherd, King, first-
born, image of God, passover lamb, etc.—and applying each
in turn to Jesus. All of them are ways of expressing faith in
Jesus. All of them underline the fact that the writers' experience of God in Christ was both much greater than anything
they had known before, and yet continuous with the past.

Each of our authors, then, interpreted Jesus in terms of his
own experience and background. It was only in this way that
any of them could express what his faith meant. The variety of
interpretation in the New Testament helps us to see that it is
possible to express the gospel in many different ways.

Read *Groundwork* 13 j–k, New Testament canon and
apocrypha.

Read *Groundwork* 40, Epilogue—History and the Gospel.

Suggestions for further reading

T. F. Glasson, *The Revelation of John* (Cambridge NEB Commentary).
* John Sweet, *Revelation* (SCM Pelican Commentary).
* John Fenton, *What was Jesus' Message?* (SPCK).
* Avery Dulles, *Apologetics and the Biblical Christ* (Burns and Oates).
David Stacey, *Interpreting the Bible* (SPCK).

Local Preachers' Studies: New Testament Study Scheme

Text-books: W. David Stacey, *Groundwork of Biblical Studies*; Morna D. Hooker, *Studying the New Testament.*

A six-monthly course is envisaged, taking a fortnight over each study. Students working by correspondence course should send the answers to two questions to the appointed tutor, beginning as soon as possible, and without further notification, after receiving the tutor's name and address. Other students may wish to use the questions for discussion in groups or for examination practice.

Study 1

Studying the New Testament
Chapter 1   The Good News about Jesus

Groundwork of Biblical Studies
Chapter 12   The languages of the Bible (b)
Chapter 15   Critical Methods
Chapter 28   Jesus

Bible passages for study:
Romans *1*.3 f.; 1 Corinthians *15*.1–8.
Mark *1*.1–13; Matthew *1–2*; Luke *1–2*; John *1*.1–18; *20*.31.

QUESTIONS
1. Why was the Old Testament important to the evangelists?
2. Why do the evangelists begin their accounts of the gospel with John the Baptist?

3. Summarize what you feel to be the vital information about Jesus which is presented by any one of the evangelists in his 'prologue'.
4. Comment on the following: Matthew *1*.22 f.; Mark *1*.7 f.; Luke *1*.32 f.; John *1*.1–3.

Study 2

Studying the New Testament
Chapter 2   'Who then is this?'—St. Mark 1.

Bible passages for study:
Mark *1*.1–*8*.30.

QUESTIONS
1. In what ways does Mark stress the authority of Jesus?
2. Why did Jesus make enemies?
3. 'Who then is this?' What answer do you feel that Mark intends us to give to this question in the miracle stories?
4. Comment on the following: Mark *2*.10; *3*.6; *4*.41; *8*.24f.

Study 3

Studying the New Testament
Chapter 3   'The Son of man must suffer'—St. Mark II

Groundwork of Biblical Studies
Chapter 31   The Synoptic Gospels (a–c)

Bible passages for study:
Mark *8*.31–*16*.8.

QUESTIONS
1. What, in Mark's understanding, does 'following Jesus' involve?
2. In what ways do you think early preachers might have used

218

the different stories which have been handed down to Mark?
3. Looking back over the whole of Mark, how would you sum up his understanding of the 'Gospel of Jesus Christ'?
4. Comment on the following: Mark 8.34; 9.5 f.; 12.10 f.; 15.37 f.

Study 4

Studying the New Testament
Chapter 4   The True Israel—St. Matthew

Groundwork of Biblical Studies
Chapter 31   The Synoptic Gospels (d–g)

Bible passages for study:
Matthew 4.1–17;   5–7;   8.1–17;   12.38–42;   16.13–22; 21.28–22.14;   23;   24.45–25.46;   27.57–28.20.

QUESTIONS
1. How does Matthew demonstrate that Jesus is greater than Moses?
2. How does Matthew underline the failure of Israel?
3. Discuss the meaning of the Lord's Prayer.
4. Comment on the following: Matthew 5.43 f.;   6.2–4; 8.10;   16.17–19.

Study 5

Studying the New Testament
Chapter 5   The Spirit of the Lord—St. Luke

Groundwork of Biblical Studies
Chapter 31   The Synoptic Gospels (h–k)
Chapter 30   The Synoptic Problem

219

Bible passages for study:
Luke *3*.1–20; *4*.14–30; *5*.1–11; *6*.17–26; *7*.11–23, 36–50; *10;* *13*.1–9; *15;* *19*.1–27; *24.*

QUESTIONS
1. In what ways does Luke demonstrate that the Holy Spirit is at work in the words and actions of Jesus?
2. Which stories in Luke would you use to illustrate the theme of repentance and forgiveness?
3. How does Luke show that the gospel is meant for outsiders?
4. Comment on the following: Luke *4*.18–21; *19*.8–10; *24*.26 f.

Study 6

Studying the New Testament
Chapter 6   The Gospel for all nations—Acts

Groundwork of Biblical Studies
Chapter 29   The Primitive Christian Community
Chapter 34   The Acts of the Apostles

Bible passages for study:
Acts *1–4;* 6; 7.44–60; *8*.1–8, 14–17, 26–40; *9–11;* *12*.1–4 *13;* *15.*

QUESTIONS
1. In what ways does Luke try to show that the Church continued 'what Jesus began to do and to teach'?
2. How does Luke interpret what happened to the disciples at Pentecost?
3. Imagine that you are an early Christian, living in Jerusalem. What would you try to say in preaching to your fellow Jews there?
4. Comment on the following: Acts *2*.4; *6*.3 f.; *10*.34 f.; *13*.2 f.

Study 7

Studying the New Testament
Chapter 7   St. Paul—Apostle to the Gentiles

Groundwork of Biblical Studies
Chapter 34   The Acts of the Apostles (c–d)
Chapter 37   The Pauline Epistles (h–i, j, m–n, q–s)

Bible passages for study:
Galatians *1.*1–17; *2.*15–21; *3.*1–*4.*11; *5.*1–6, 13–25.
Philippians *1.*27–*2.*15; *3.*1–21.
1 Thessalonians *1*; *4.*1–*5.*11.

QUESTIONS
1. Why did Paul feel so strongly about those who opposed him in the Galatian churches? Was he right?
2. 'All Paul's theological argument is based on his understanding of the gospel–Christ crucified and risen.' Is this true of the three epistles you have been studying?
3. Do you think that what Paul wrote to the Thessalonian church has any relevance today?
4. Comment on the following: Galatians *1.*1; *4.*4–7; Philippians *2.*5–8; *3.*20–1.

Study 8

Studying the New Testament
Chapter 8   St. Paul—Pastor of the Churches

Groundwork of Biblical Studies
Chapter 37   The Pauline Epistles (d–g)

Bible passages for study:
1 Corinthians *1.*1–*2.*5;   *3.*1–17;   *11.*17–26;   *12;   13;

14.1–19, 26–33; *15*.1–28, 35–37.
2 Corinthians *1*.1–17; *4*.5–12, 16–18; *5*; *6*.1–10.

QUESTIONS
1. How did Paul approach social and ethical problems?
2. Paul says that the greatest gift of the Spirit is love; in what ways were the Corinthians failing to show love?
3. What, according to Paul, should be the characteristics of the life and work of a minister of the gospel?
4. Comment on the following: 1 Corinthians *1*.25–7; *3*.1–4; *11*.23–6; 2 Corinthians *4*.10–12.

Study 9

Studying the New Testament
Chapter 9   St. Paul—Theologian

Groundwork of Biblical Studies
Chapter 37   The Pauline Epistles (a–c, o–p, k–l)

Bible passages for study:
Romans *1*.1–6, 16–17; *3*.21–8; *5*; *6*.1–14; *8*; *9*.1–5; *10*.1–4; *11*.1–6, 25–36.
Colossians *1*.13–20; *3*.1–17.
Ephesians *1*.3–14; 2.11–22; 6.10.20.

QUESTIONS
1. Outline what Paul says in his letters about the work of the Spirit.
2. What do we learn from Paul's letters about his hope for the future?
3. What does Paul mean by union with Christ, and why is it so important?
4. Comment on the following: Romans *3*.21–5; *6*.1–4; Colossians *1*.15–17; Ephesians 2.11–14.

Study 10

Studying the New Testament
Chapter 10   Letters from other Leaders

Groundwork of Biblical Studies
Chapter 38   The General Epistles
Chapter 37   The Pauline Epistles (t–v)

Bible passages for study:
Hebrews *1*.1–5;   *2*.10–18;   *4*.14–*5*.10;   *7*.26–*8*.6;
9.11–14, 23–28; *10*.1–25; *11*.1–3.
James *2*.
1 Peter *1*.1–*3*.12;   *4*.12–19.
1 John.
1 Timothy *3*.14–16.
2 Timothy *2*.1–15;   *4*.1–8.

QUESTIONS
1. How does the author of Hebrews try to express the uniqueness of Christ?
2. What encouragement does 1 Peter offer to those facing persecution?
3. How would you sum up the message of 1 John?
4. Comment on the following: Hebrews *10*.11 f.; James *2*.18; 1 Peter *1*.18 f.; 1 John *4*.2 f.

Study 11

Studying the New Testament
Chapter 11   The Spiritual Gospel—St. John

Groundwork of Biblical Studies
Chapter 32   The Fourth Gospel

Bible passages for study:
John *1*.19–*3*.21;   *4*.4–42;   *5*.19–47;   *6*.22–71;   *9*.1–*10*.18;
11.1–54; *12*.20–36; *13*.1–30; *14*; *15*; *17*; *18*.33–8; *20*; *21*.

223

QUESTIONS

1. How does John use the actions of Jesus to teach us about who he is?
2. What does John mean by 'eternal life'?
3. What does John's gospel teach about the Holy Spirit?
4. Comment on the following: John *1*.29 f.; *3*.14; *4*.13 f.; *15*.1 f.

Study 12

Studying the New Testament
Chapter 12   A Faith for all Times

Groundwork of Biblical Studies
Chapter 13   The Canon (j–k)
Chapter 39   Revelation
Chapter 20   Literary Types in the Old Testament (1)
Chapter 40   Epilogue—History and the Gospel

Bible passages for study:
Revelation *1*; *7*; *21*.1–22.5.

QUESTIONS

1. Which New Testament book that you have studied have you found the most helpful in understanding your own Christian experience, and why?
2. What do Christians hope for? Do you find the book of Revelation a helpful way of expressing it?
3. Do you feel that critical study of the New Testament raises any problems for Christians?
4. What would you reply to someone who said that the language and ideas of the New Testament are irrelevant today?